CIMA

PRACTICE & REVISION KIT
COMPUTER BASED
ASSESSMENT

Foundation Paper 1

Financial Accounting
Fundamentals

BPP Professional Education
January 2004

First edition 2001
Fourth edition January 2004

ISBN 0 7517 1498 4 (previous edition 0 7517 0273 0)

British Library Cataloguing-in-Publication Data
A catalogue record for this book
is available from the British Library

Published by

BPP Professional Education
Aldine House, Aldine Place
London W12 8AW

www.bpp.com

Printed in Great Britain by W M Print
45-47 Frederick Street
Walsall WS2 9NE

We are grateful to the Chartered Institute of Management Accountants for permission to reproduce past examination questions. The answers to past examination questions have been prepared by BPP Professional Education.

CONTENTS

Order form

Review form & free prize draw

BPP
PROFESSIONAL EDUCATION

REVISING WITH THIS KIT

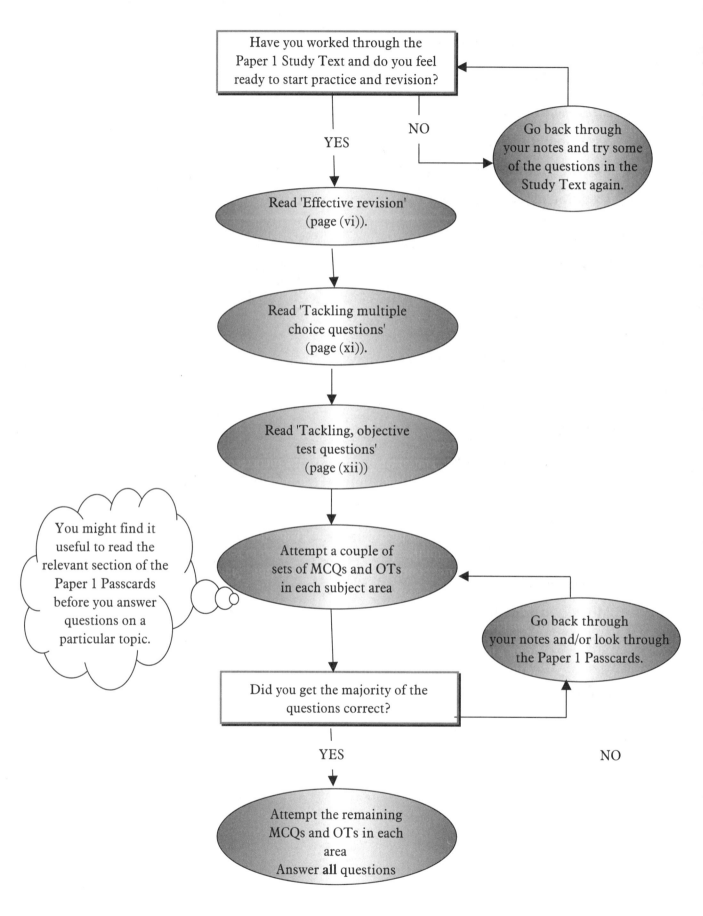

Have you worked through the Paper 1 Study Text and do you feel ready to start practice and revision?

NO → Go back through your notes and try some of the questions in the Study Text again.

YES ↓

Read 'Effective revision' (page (vi)).

Read 'Tackling multiple choice questions' (page (xi)).

Read 'Tackling, objective test questions' (page (xii))

You might find it useful to read the relevant section of the Paper 1 Passcards before you answer questions on a particular topic.

Attempt a couple of sets of MCQs and OTs in each subject area

Go back through your notes and/or look through the Paper 1 Passcards.

Did you get the majority of the questions correct?

YES ↓   NO →

Attempt the remaining MCQs and OTs in each area
Answer **all** questions

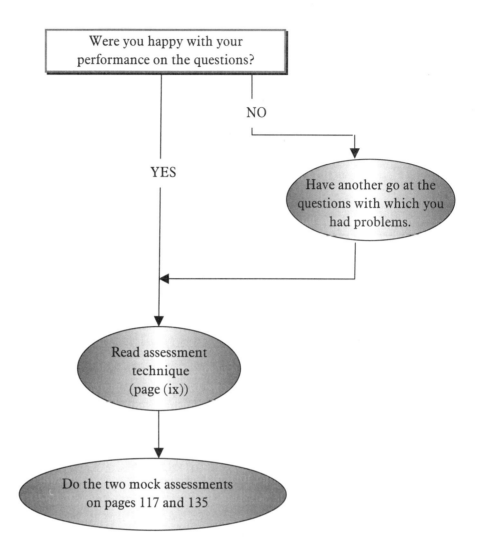

Were you happy with your performance on the questions?

NO

YES

Have another go at the questions with which you had problems.

Read assessment technique (page (ix))

Do the two mock assessments on pages 117 and 135

BPP
PROFESSIONAL EDUCATION

EFFECTIVE REVISION

This guidance applies if you have been studying for an exam over a period of time. (Some tuition providers are teaching subjects by means of one intensive course that ends with the assessment.)

What you must remember

Time is very important as you approach the assessment. You must remember:

> **Believe in yourself**
> **Use time sensibly**

> **Believe in yourself**

Are you cultivating the right attitude of mind? There is absolutely no reason why you should not pass this **assessment** if you adopt the correct approach.

- **Be confident** – you've passed exams before, you can pass them again
- **Be calm** – plenty of adrenaline but no panicking
- **Be focused** – commit yourself to passing the assessment

> **Use time sensibly**

1   **How much study time do you have?** Remember that you must EAT, SLEEP, and of course, RELAX.

2   **How will you split that available time between each subject?** A revision timetable, covering what and how you will revise, will help you organise your revision thoroughly.

3   **What is your learning style?** AM/PM? Little and often/long sessions? Evenings/ weekends?

4   **Do you have quality study time?** Unplug the phone. Let everybody know that you're studying and shouldn't be disturbed.

5   **Are you taking regular breaks?** Most people absorb more if they do not attempt to study for long uninterrupted periods of time. A five minute break every hour (to make coffee, watch the news headlines) can make all the difference.

6   **Are you rewarding yourself for your hard work?** Are you leading a **healthy lifestyle?**

What to revise

> **Key topics**

You need to spend **most time** on, and practise **lots of questions** on, topics that are likely to yield plenty of questions in your assessment.

You may also find certain areas of the syllabus difficult.

> Difficult areas are
>
> - Areas you find dull or pointless
> - Subjects you highlighted as difficult when you studied them
> - Topics that gave you problems when you answered questions or reviewed the material

DON'T become depressed about these areas; instead do something about them.

- Build up your knowledge by **quick tests** such as the quick quizzes in your BPP Study Text and the MCQ cards.

- Work carefully through **numerical examples** and **questions** in the Text, and refer back to the Text if you struggle with questions in the Kit.

Breadth of revision

Make sure your revision covers all areas of the syllabus. Your assessment will test your knowledge of the whole syllabus.

How to revise

There are four main ways that you can revise a topic area.

Write it!
Read it!
Teach it!
Do it!

Write it!

Writing important points down will help you recall them, particularly if your notes are presented in a way that makes it easy for you to remember them.

Read it!

You should read your notes or BPP Passcards actively, testing yourself by doing quick quizzes or Kit questions while you are reading.

Teach it!

Assessments require you to show your understanding. Teaching what you are learning to another person helps you practise explaining topics that you might be asked to define in your assessment. Teaching someone who will challenge your understanding, someone for example who will be taking the same assessment as you, can be helpful to both of you.

Do it!

Remember that you are revising in order to be able to answer questions in the assessment. Practising questions will help you practise **technique** and **discipline**, which can be crucial in passing or failing assessments.

1   Start your question practice by doing a couple of sets of multiple choice questions and objective test questions in a subject area. Note down the questions where you went wrong, try to identify why you made mistakes and go back to your Study Text for guidance or practice.

2   The **more questions** you do, the more likely you are to pass the assessment. However if you do run short of time:

- Make sure that you have done at least some questions from every section of the syllabus

- Look through the banks of multiple choice questions and objective test questions and do questions on areas that you have found difficult or on which you have made mistakes

3   When you think you can successfully answer questions on the whole syllabus, attempt the **two mock assessments** at the end of the Kit. You will get the most benefit by sitting them under strict assessment conditions, so that you gain experience of the vital assessment processes.

- Managing your time
- Producing answers

BPP's *Learning to Learn Accountancy* gives further valuable advice on how to approach revision.

BPP has also produced other vital revision aids.

- **Passcards** – Provide you with clear topic summaries and assessment tips

- **MCQ Cards** – Prepare you for answering multiple choice questions by giving you lots and lots of practice

- **i-Pass CDs** – Offer you tests of knowledge to be completed against the clock

- **Success Tapes and Success CDs** – Help you revise on the move

You can purchase these products by completing the order form at the back of this Kit or by visiting www.bpp.com/cima

---

ASSESSMENT TECHNIQUE

Format of the assessment

The assessment will contain 40 questions to be completed in 1½ hours. The questions will be a combination of multiple choice questions and other types of objective test questions.

Passing assessments

Passing assessments is half about having the knowledge, and half about doing yourself full justice in the assessment. You must have the right approach to two things.

> **The day of the assessment**
>
> **Your time in the assessment room**

The day of the assessment

1   Set at least one **alarm** (or get an alarm call) for a morning assessment.

2   Have **something to eat** but beware of eating too much; you may feel sleepy if your system is digesting a large meal.

3   Allow plenty of **time to get to the assessment room**; have your route worked out in advance and listen to news bulletins to check for potential travel problems.

4   **Don't forget** pens and watch. Also make sure you remember **entrance documentation** and **evidence of identity**.

5   Put **new batteries** into your calculator and take a spare set (or a spare calculator).

6   **Avoid discussion** about the assessment with other candidates outside the assessment room.

Your time in the assessment room

1   *Listen carefully to the invigilator's instructions*

Make sure you understand the formalities you have to complete.

2   *Ensure you follow the instructions on the computer screen*

In particular ensure that you select the correct assessment (not every student does!), and that you understand how to work through the assessment and submit your answers.

3   *Keep your eye on the time*

In the assessment you will have to complete 40 questions in 90 minutes. That will mean that you have roughly 2 minutes on average to answer each question. However you will be able to answer some questions instantly, but others will require working out. If after a couple of minutes you have no idea how to tackle the question, leave it and come back to it later.

4   *Label your workings clearly with the question number*

This will help you when you check your answers, or if you come back to a question that you are unsure about.

5   *Deal with problem questions*

There are two ways of dealing with questions where you are unsure of the answer.

(a) **Don't submit an answer.** The computer will tell you before you move to the next question that you have not submitted an answer, and the question will be marked as not done on the list of questions. The risk with this approach is that you run out of time before you do submit an answer.

(b) **Submit an answer.** You can always come back and change the answer before you finish the assessment or the time runs out. You should though make a note of answers that you are unsure about, to ensure that you do revisit them later in the assessment.

6   *Make sure you submit an answer for every question*

When there are ten minutes left to go, concentrate on submitting answers for all the questions that you have not answered up to that point. You won't get penalised for wrong answers so take a guess if you're unsure.

7   *Check your answers*

If you finish the assessment with time to spare, check your answers before you sign out of the assessment. In particular revisit questions that you are unsure about, and check that your answers are in the right format and contain the correct number of words as appropriate.

BPP's *Learning to Learn Accountancy* gives further valuable advice on how to approach the day of the assessment.

TACKLING MULTIPLE CHOICE QUESTIONS

The MCQs in your assessment contain a number of possible answers. You have to **choose the option(s) that best answers the question**. The three incorrect options are called distracters. There is a skill in answering MCQs quickly and correctly. By practising MCQs you can develop this skill, giving you a better chance of passing the assessment.

You may wish to follow the approach outlined below, or you may prefer to adapt it.

Step 1. **Note down how long** you should allocate to each MCQ. For this paper you will be answering 40 questions in 90 minutes, so you will be spending on average just over two minutes on each question. Remember however that you will not be expected to spend an equal amount of time on each MCQ; some can be answered instantly but others will take time to work out.

Step 2. **Attempt each question**. Read the question thoroughly.

You may find that you recognise a question when you sit the assessment. Be aware that the detail and/or requirement may be different. If the question seems familiar read the requirement and options carefully – do not assume that it is identical.

Step 3. Read the four options and see if one matches your own answer. Be careful with numerical questions, as the distracters are designed to match answers that incorporate **common errors**. Check that your calculation is correct. Have you followed the requirement exactly? Have you included every stage of the calculation?

Step 4. You may find that none of the options matches your answer.

- **Re-read the question** to ensure that you understand it and are answering the requirement

- **Eliminate any obviously wrong answers**

- **Consider which of the remaining answers** is the **most likely** to be correct and select the option

Step 5. If you are still unsure, **continue to the next question**. Likewise if you are nowhere near working out which option is correct after a couple of minutes, leave the question and come back to it later. Make a note of any questions for which you have submitted answers, but you need to return to later. The computer will list any questions for which you have not submitted answers.

Step 6. **Revisit questions** you are uncertain about. When you come back to a question after a break you often find you are able to answer it correctly straight away. If you are still unsure have a guess. You are not penalised for incorrect answers, so **never leave a question unanswered!**

TACKLING OBJECTIVE TEST QUESTIONS

What is an objective test question?

An objective test (**OT**) question is made up of some form of **stimulus**, usually a question, and a **requirement** to do something.

- **MCQs.** Read through the information on page (xi) about MCQs and how to tackle them.

- **Data entry.** This type of OT requires you to provide figures such as the correct figure for creditors in a balance sheet.

- **Hot spots.** This question format might ask you to identify which cell on a spreadsheet contains a particular formula or where on a graph marginal revenue equals marginal cost.

- **Multiple response.** These questions provide you with a number of options and you have to identify those that fulfil certain criteria.

- **Matching.** This OT question format could ask you to classify particular costs into one of a range of cost classifications provided, to match descriptions of variances with one of a number of variances listed, and so on.

OT questions in your assessment

CIMA is currently developing different types of OTs for inclusion in computer-based assessments. The timetable for introduction of new types of OTs is uncertain, and it is also not certain how many questions in your assessment will be MCQs, and how many will be other types of OT. Practising all the different types of OTs that this Kit provides will prepare you well for whatever questions come up in your assessment.

Dealing with OT questions

Again you may wish to follow the approach we suggest, or you may be prepared to adapt it.

Step 1.   Work out **how long** you should allocate to each OT. Remember that you will not be expected to spend an equal amount of time on each one; some can be answered instantly but others will take time to work out.

Step 2.   **Attempt each question.** Read the question thoroughly, and note in particular what the question says about the **format** of your answer and whether there are any **restrictions** placed on it (for example the number of words you can use).

           You may find that you recognise a question when you sit the assessment. Be aware that the detail and/or requirement may be different. If the question seems familiar read the requirement and options carefully – do not assume that it is identical.

Step 3.   Read any options you are given and select which ones are appropriate. Check that your calculations are correct. Have you followed the requirement exactly? Have you included every stage of the calculation?

Step 4.   You may find that you are unsure of the answer.

- Re-read the question to ensure that you understand it and are answering the requirement

- Eliminate any obviously wrong options if you are given a number of options from which to choose

- Consider which of any remaining answers is the most likely to be correct and select the option

Step 5. If you are still unsure, **continue to the next question**. Make a note of any questions for which you have submitted answers, but you need to return to later. The computer will list any questions for which you have not submitted answers.

Step 6. Revisit questions you are uncertain about. When you come back to a question after a break you often find you are able to answer it correctly straight away. If you are still unsure have a guess. You are not penalised for incorrect answers, so **never leave a question unanswered!**

USEFUL WEBSITES

The websites below provide additional sources of information of relevance to your studies for *Financial Accounting Fundamentals*.

- BPP   www.bpp.com

  For details of other BPP material for your CIMA studies

- CIMA   www.cimaglobal.com

  The official CIMA website

- *Financial Times*   www.ft.com

  Essential background reading, as recommended by the examiner

- *The Economist*   www.economist.com

  Background material as recommended by the examiner

- *Financial pages of TV sites*   www.bbc.co.uk

  www.msnbc.com

  www.cnn.com

- *Customs & Excise (VAT)*   www.hmce.gov.uk

- *Inland Revenue (PAYE)*   www.inlandrevenue.gov.uk

CURRENT ISSUES

Update to *Financial Accounting Fundamentals* study text.

Chapter 2 – Preparing accounts: concepts, conventions and regulations.

Please note the following regarding **FRS 18**.

The old SSAP 2 identified four fundamental accounting concepts – going concern, accruals, prudence and consistency.

FRS 18 focuses upon **accruals** and **going concern** as **bedrocks** of accounting. The other two concepts – prudence and consistency – are described in FRS 18 as simply **desirable features** of financial statements. The SSAP 2 idea that 'prudence prevails', that the most pessimistic outcome should always be provided for, has been replaced by the objective of 'neutrality' – the information presented should be free from bias.

FRS 18 also specifies that accounting policies should be selected which ensure that financial statements have:

- Relevance
- Reliability
- Comparability
- Understandability

Another term used in FRS 18 is **estimation techniques**, sometimes called accounting estimates. These involve the use of judgement when applying accounting policies. For instance, the accounting policy may state that fixed assets are depreciated over their expected useful life. The decision regarding the length of useful life is a matter of **estimation**. The decision regarding method of depreciation is also a matter of estimation, rather than accounting policy.

There is the further matter of **measurement bases**. Is the value of the asset, upon which its depreciation is based, stated at original cost or revalued amount? This is the measurement basis and will be stated in the accounting policy. For instance, a change of stock valuation policy from weighted average to FIFO would be a change of measurement basis *and* a change of accounting policy.

The company must disclose in the notes to the accounts any change of accounting policy. Any change of **measurement basis** is regarded as a change of accounting policy and must be disclosed. Any change of **presentation** (how items are presented in the accounts) is a change of accounting policy. Any change in **estimation technique** is not a change of accounting policy and need not be disclosed.

Question 7 on page 19 of the study text should be disregarded.

SYLLABUS MINDMAP

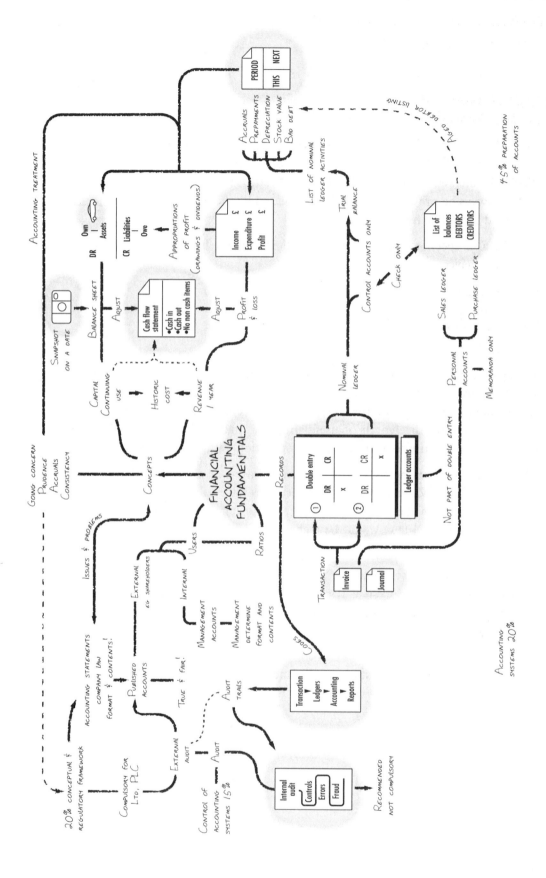

QUESTION AND ANSWER CHECKLIST/INDEX

The headings in this checklist/index indicate the main topics of questions, but questions often cover several different topics.

BPP
PROFESSIONAL EDUCATION

Question and answer checklist/index

Questions

Multiple choice questions

1   CONCEPTUAL AND REGULATORY FRAMEWORK

1   The historical cost convention

    A   Fails to take account of changing price levels over time

    B   Records only past transactions

    C   Values all assets at their cost to the business, without any adjustment for depreciation

    D   Has been replaced in accounting records by a system of current cost accounting

2   The *main* aim of accounting is to

    A   Maintain ledger accounts for every asset and liability

    B   Provide financial information to users of such information

    C   Produce a trial balance

    D   Record every financial transaction individually

3   The accounting convention under which items in the accounts are adjusted by reference to the Retail Price Index is known as

    A   Current cost accounting

    B   Historical cost accounting

    C   Alternative accounting rules

    D   Current purchasing power accounting

4   In the time of rising prices, the historical cost convention has the effect of

    A   Understating profits and understating balance sheet asset values

    B   Understating profits and overstating balance sheet asset values

    C   Overstating profits and understating balance sheet asset values

    D   Overstating profits and overstating balance sheet asset values

5   The accounting equation can be rewritten as

    A   Assets plus profit less drawings less liabilities equals closing capital

    B   Assets less liabilities less drawings equals opening capital plus profit

    C   Assets less liabilities less opening capital plus drawings equals profit

    D   Opening capital plus profit less drawings less liabilities equals assets

6   If the owner of a business takes goods from stock for his own personal use, the accounting concept to be considered is the

    A   Prudence concept

    B   Capitalisation concept

    C   Money measurement concept

    D   Separate entity concept

7   Which of the following best explains what is meant by 'capital expenditure'?

Capital expenditure is expenditure

    A   On fixed assets, including repairs and maintenance

    B   On expensive assets

    C   Relating to the issue of share capital

    D   Relating to the acquisition or improvement of fixed assets

8   Sales revenue should be recognised when goods and services have been supplied; costs are incurred when goods and services have been received.

The accounting concept which governs the above is the

A   Accruals concept
B   Materiality concept
C   Realisation concept
D   Dual aspect concept

9   The capital maintenance concept implies that

A   The capital of a business should be kept intact by not paying out dividends

B   A business should invest its profits in the purchase of capital assets

C   Fixed assets should be properly maintained

D   Profit is earned only if the value of an organisation's net assets or its operating capability has increased during the accounting period

10 In times of rising prices, the historical cost convention:

A   Understates asset values and profits
B   Understates asset values and overstates profits
C   Overstates asset values and profits
D   Overstates asset values and understates profits

2   DOUBLE ENTRY BOOKKEEPING I

1   Gross profit for 20X3 can be calculated from

A   Purchases for 20X3, plus stock at 31 December 20X3, less stock at 1 January 20X3

B   Purchases for 20X3, less stock at 31 December 20X3, plus stock at 1 January 20X3

C   Cost of goods sold during 20X3, plus sales during 20X3

D   Net profit for 20X3, plus expenses for 20X3

2   Rent paid on 1 October 20X2 for the year to 30 September 20X3 was £1,200, and rent paid on 1 October 20X3 for the year to 30 September 20X4 was £1,600.

Rent payable, as shown in the profit and loss account for the year ended 31 December 20X3, would be

A   £1,200
B   £1,600
C   £1,300
D   £1,500

3   A decrease in the provision for doubtful debts would result in

A   An increase in liabilities
B   A decrease in working capital
C   A decrease in net profit
D   An increase in net profit

4   If, at the end of the financial year, a company makes a charge against the profits for stationery consumed but not yet invoiced, this adjustment is in accordance with the concept of

A   Materiality
B   Accruals
C   Consistency
D   Objectivity

5   A credit balance of £917 brought down on Y Ltd's account in the books of X Ltd means that

A   X Ltd owes Y Ltd £917
B   Y Ltd owes X Ltd £917
C   X Ltd has paid Y Ltd £917
D   X Ltd is owed £917 by Y Ltd

6   A company received an invoice from ABC Ltd, for 40 units at £10 each, less 25% trade discount, these being items purchased on credit and for resale. It paid this invoice minus a cash discount of 2%. Which of the following journal entries correctly records the effect of the whole transaction in the company's books?

		Debit £	Credit £
A	ABC Ltd	300	
	Purchases		300
	Cash	292	
	Discount allowed	8	
	ABC Ltd		300
B	Purchases	300	
	ABC Ltd		300
	ABC Ltd	300	
	Discount allowed		8
	Cash		292
C	Purchases	300	
	ABC Ltd		300
	ABC Ltd	300	
	Discount received		6
	Cash		294
D	ABC Ltd	400	
	Purchases		400
	Cash	294	
	Discount received	106	
	ABC Ltd		400

7   The following is an extract from the trial balance of ABC Ltd at 31 December 20X4.

	Debit £	Credit £
Sales		73,716
Returns	5,863	3,492
Discounts	871	1,267

7

The figure to be shown in the trading account for net sales is

A   £66,586
B   £66,982
C   £67,853
D   £70,224

8   From the following information, calculate the value of purchases.

	£
Opening creditors	142,600
Cash paid	542,300
Discounts received	13,200
Goods returned	27,500
Closing creditors	137,800

A   £302,600
B   £506,400
C   £523,200
D   £578,200

9   Net profit was calculated as being £10,200. It was later discovered that capital expenditure of £3,000 had been treated as revenue expenditure, and revenue receipts of £1,400 had been treated as capital receipts.

The correct net profit should have been

A   £5,800
B   £8,600
C   £11,800
D   £14,600

10   Stationery paid for during 20X5 amounted to £1,350. At the beginning of 20X5 there was a stock of stationery on hand of £165 and an outstanding invoice for £80. At the end of 20X5, there was a stock of stationery on hand of £140 and an outstanding invoice for £70. The stationery figure to be shown in the profit and loss account for 20X5 is

A   £1,195
B   £1,335
C   £1,365
D   £1,505

3   DOUBLE ENTRY BOOKKEEPING II

1   An increase in stock of £250, a decrease in the bank balance of £400 and an increase in creditors of £1,200 result in

A   A decrease in working capital of £1,350
B   An increase in working capital of £1,350
C   A decrease in working capital of £1,050
D   An increase in working capital of £1,050

2   A credit balance on a ledger account indicates

   A   An asset or an expense
   B   A liability or an expense
   C   An amount owing to the organisation
   D   A liability or a revenue

3   Which ONE of the following is not a book of prime entry?

   A   The petty cash book
   B   The sales returns day book
   C   The sales ledger
   D   The cash book

4   A book of prime entry is one in which

   A   The rules of double-entry bookkeeping do not apply
   B   Ledger accounts are maintained
   C   Transactions are entered prior to being recorded in the ledger account
   D   Subsidiary accounts are kept

5   A business has opening stock of £12,000 and closing stock of £18,000. Purchase returns were £5,000. The cost of goods sold was £111,000.

   Purchases were

   A   £100,000
   B   £110,000
   C   £116,000
   D   £122,000

6   The double-entry system of bookkeeping normally results in which of the following balances on the ledger accounts?

	Debit balances	*Credit balances*
A	Assets and revenues	Liabilities, capital and expenses
B	Revenues, capital and liabilities	Assets and expenses
C	Assets and expenses	Liabilities, capital and revenues
D	Assets, expenses and capital	Liabilities and revenues

7   A business commenced with capital in cash of £1,000. Stock costing £800 is purchased on credit, and half is sold for £1,000 plus VAT, the customer paying in cash at once.

   The accounting equation after these transactions would show:

   A   Assets £1,775 less Liabilities £175 equals Capital £1,600
   B   Assets £2,175 less Liabilities £975 equals Capital £1,200
   C   Assets £2,575 less Liabilities £800 equals Capital £1,775
   D   Assets £2,575 less Liabilities £975 equals Capital £1,600

8   A sole trader had opening capital of £10,000 and closing capital of £4,500. During the period, the owner introduced capital of £4,000 and withdrew £8,000 for her own use.

Her profit or loss during the period was

A   £9,500 loss
B   £1,500 loss
C   £7,500 profit
D   £17,500 profit

9   A credit entry of £450 on X's account in the books of Y could have arisen by

A   X buying goods on credit from Y
B   Y paying X £450
C   Y returning goods to X
D   X returning goods to Y

10 At 1 September, the motor expenses account showed 4-months' insurance prepaid of £80 and petrol accrued of £95. During September, the outstanding petrol bill is paid, plus further bills of £245. At 30 September there is a further outstanding petrol bill of £120.

The amount to be shown in the profit and loss account for motor expenses for September is

A   £385
B   £415
C   £445
D   £460

4   STOCKS

1   In times of rising prices, the FIFO method of stock valuation, when compared to the average cost method of stock valuation, will usually produce

A   A higher profit and a lower closing stock value
B   A higher profit and a higher closing stock value
C   A lower profit and a lower closing stock value
D   A lower profit and a higher closing stock value

2   Following the preparation of the profit and loss account, it is discovered that accrued expenses of £1,000 have been ignored and that closing stock has been overvalued by £1,300. This will have resulted in

A   An overstatement of net profit of £300
B   An understatement of net profit of £300
C   An overstatement of net profit of £2,300
D   An understatement of net profit of £2,300

3   Stock is valued using FIFO. Opening stock was 10 units at £2 each. Purchases were 30 units at £3 each, then issues of 12 units were made, followed by issues of 8 units.

Closing stock is valued at

A   £50
B   £58
C   £60
D   £70

4   An organisation's stock at 1 July is 15 units @ £3.00 each. The following movements occur:

- 3 July 20X6   5 units sold at £3.30 each
- 8 July 20X6   10 units bought at £3.50 each
- 12 July 20X6   8 units sold at £4.00 each

Closing stock at 31 July, using the FIFO method of stock valuation would be

A   £31.50
B   £36.00
C   £39.00
D   £41.00

5   Your organisation uses the weighted average cost method of valuing stocks. During August 20X1, the following stock details were recorded:

Opening balance   30 units valued at £2 each
5 August   purchase of 50 units at £2.40 each
10 August   issue of 40 units
18 August   purchase of 60 units at £2.50 each
23 August   issue of 25 units

The value of the balance at 31 August 20X1 was

A   £172.50
B   £176.25
C   £180.00
D   £187.50

6   During September, your organisation had sales of £148,000, which made a gross profit of £40,000. Purchases amounted to £100,000 and opening stock was £34,000.

The value of closing stock was

A   £24,000
B   £26,000
C   £42,000
D   £54,000

7   Your firm values stock using the weighted average cost method. At 1 October 20X8, there were 60 units in stock valued at £12 each. On 8 October , 40 units were purchased for £15 each, and a further 50 units were purchased for £18 each on 14 October. On 21 October, 75 units were sold for £1,200.

The value of closing stock at 31 October 20X8 was:

A   £900
B   £1,020
C   £1,110
D   £1,125

8   Stock movements for product X during the last quarter were as follows:

January	Purchases	10 items at £19.80 each
February	Sales	10 items at £30 each
March	Purchases	20 items at £24.50 each
	Sales	5 items at £30 each

Opening stock at 1 January was 6 items valued at £15 each

Gross profit for the quarter, using the weighted average cost method, would be

A   £135.75
B   £155.00
C   £174.00
D   £483.00

9   In times of rising prices, the valuation of stock using the FIFO method, as opposed to average cost, will result in which ONE of the following combinations?

	Cost of sales	*Profit*	*Closing stocks*
A	Lower	Higher	Higher
B	Lower	Higher	Lower
C	Higher	Lower	Higher
D	Higher	Higher	Lower

10   Which of the following methods of valuing stocks are allowed under SSAP 9.

(i)   LIFO
(ii)   Average cost
(iii) FIFO
(iv)   Replacement cost

A   (i), (ii), (iii), (iv)
B   (i), (ii), (iv)
C   (ii), (iii)
D   (iii), (iv)

5   FIXED ASSETS

1   What is the purpose of charging depreciation in accounts?

    A   To allocate the cost less residual value of a fixed asset over the accounting periods expected to benefit from its use

    B   To ensure that funds are available for the eventual replacement of the asset

    C   To reduce the cost of the asset in the balance sheet to its estimated market value

    D   To comply with the prudence concept

2   Your firm bought a machine for £5,000 on 1 January 20X1, which had an expected useful life of four years and an expected residual value of £1,000; the asset was to be depreciated on the straight-line basis. On 31 December 20X3, the machine was sold for £1,600.

The amount to be entered in the 20X3 profit and loss account for profit or loss on disposal, is

    A   Profit of £600
    B   Loss of £600
    C   Profit of £350
    D   Loss of £400

3   A fixed asset register showed a net book value of £67,460. A fixed asset costing £15,000 had been sold for £4,000, making a loss on disposal of £1,250. No entries had been made in the fixed asset register for this disposal.

The balance on the fixed asset register should be

    A   £42,710
    B   £51,210
    C   £53,710
    D   £62,210

4   An organisation's fixed asset register shows a net book value of £135,600. The fixed asset account in the nominal ledger shows a net book value of £125,600. The difference could be due to a disposed asset not having been removed from the fixed asset ledger.

    A   With disposal proceeds of £15,000 and a profit on disposal of £5,000
    B   With disposal proceeds of £15,000 and a net book value of £5,000
    C   With disposal proceeds of £15,000 and a loss on disposal of £5,000
    D   With disposal proceeds of £5,000 and a net book value of £5,000

5   Recording the purchase of computer stationery by debiting the computer equipment account at cost would result in

    A   An overstatement of profit and an overstatement of fixed assets
    B   An understatement of profit and an overstatement of fixed assets
    C   An overstatement of profit and an understatement of fixed assets
    D   An understatement of profit and an understatement of fixed assets

6   Depreciation is best described as

    A   A means of spreading the payment for fixed assets over a period of years
    B   A decline in the market value of the assets
    C   A means of spreading the net cost of fixed assets over their estimated useful life
    D   A means of estimating the amount of money needed to replace the assets

7   A business has made a profit of £8,000 but its bank balance has fallen by £5,000. This could be due to

   A   Depreciation of £3,000 and an increase in stocks of £10,000
   B   Depreciation of £6,000 and the repayment of a loan of £7,000
   C   Depreciation of £12,000 and the purchase of new fixed assets for £25,000
   D   The disposal of a fixed asset for £13,000 less than its book value

8   A fixed asset costing £12,500 was sold at a book loss of £4,500. Depreciation had been provided using the reducing balance, at 20% per annum since its purchase.

   Which of the following correctly describes the sale proceeds and length of time for which the asset had been owned?

	Sale proceeds	*Length of ownership*
A	Cannot be calculated	Cannot be calculated
B	Cannot be calculated	2 years
C	£8,000	Cannot be calculated
D	£8,000	2 years

9   On 1 July 20X7, your fixed asset register showed a net book value of £47,500. The ledger accounts showed fixed assets at cost of £60,000 and provision for depreciation of £15,000. It was discovered that the disposal of an asset for £4,000, giving rise to a loss on disposal of £1,500, had not been recorded in the fixed asset register.

   After correcting this omission, the fixed asset register would show a balance which was

   A   £3,000 lower than the ledger accounts
   B   £1,500 lower than the ledger accounts
   C   equal to the ledger accounts
   D   £1,000 higher than the ledger accounts

10 A fixed asset was purchased at the beginning of Year 1 for £2,400 and depreciated by 20% per annum by the reducing balance method. At the beginning of Year 4 it was sold for £1,200. The result of this was

   A   A loss on disposal of £240.00
   B   A loss on disposal of £28.80
   C   A profit on disposal of £28.80
   D   A profit on disposal of £240.00

6   BANK RECONCILIATIONS

1   Your cash book at 31 December 20X3 shows a bank balance of £565 overdrawn. On comparing this with your bank statement at the same date, you discover the following.

   (a)   A cheque for £57 drawn by you on 29 December 20X3 has not yet been presented for payment.

   (b)   A cheque for £92 from a customer, which was paid into the bank on 24 December 20X3, has been dishonoured on 31 December 20X3.

   The correct bank balance to be shown in the balance sheet at 31 December 20X3 is

   A   £714 overdrawn
   B   £657 overdrawn
   C   £473 overdrawn
   D   £53 overdrawn

14

2   The cash book shows a bank balance of £5,675 overdrawn at 31 August 20X5. It is subsequently discovered that a standing order for £125 has been entered twice, and that a dishonoured cheque for £450 has been debited in the cash book instead of credited.

The correct bank balance should be

A   £5,100 overdrawn
B   £6,000 overdrawn
C   £6,250 overdrawn
D   £6,450 overdrawn

3   A business had a balance at the bank of £2,500 at the start of the month. During the following month, it paid for materials invoiced at £1,000 less trade discount of 20% and cash discount of 10%. It received a cheque from a debtor in respect of an invoice for £200, subject to cash discount of 5%.

The balance at the bank at the end of the month was

A   £1,970
B   £1,980
C   £1,990
D   £2,000

4   The bank statement on 31 October 20X7 showed an overdraft of £800. On reconciling the bank statement, it was discovered that a cheque drawn by your company for £80 had not been presented for payment, and that a cheque for £130 from a customer had been dishonoured on 30 October 20X7.

The correct bank balance to be shown in the balance sheet at 31 October 20X7 is

A   £1,010 overdrawn
B   £880 overdrawn
C   £750 overdrawn
D   £720 overdrawn

5   Your firm's cash book at 30 April 20X8 shows a balance at the bank of £2,490. Comparison with the bank statement at the same date reveals the following differences:

	£
Unpresented cheques	840
Bank charges not in cash book	50
Receipts not yet credited by the bank	470
Dishonoured cheque not in cash book	140

The correct balance on the cash book at 30 April 20X8 is

A   £1,460
B   £2,300
C   £2,580
D   £3,140

6   Your firm's bank statement at 31 October 20X8 shows a balance of £13,400. You subsequently discover that the bank has dishonoured a customer's cheque for £300 and has charged bank charges of £50, neither of which is recorded in your cash book. There are unpresented cheques totalling £2,400. Amounts paid in, but not yet credited by the bank, amount to £1,000. You further discover that an automatic receipt from a customer of £195 has been recorded as a credit in your cash book.

Your cash book balance, prior to correcting the errors and omissions, was:

A £11,455

B £11,960

C £12,000

D £12,155

7   Your firm's cashbook shows a credit bank balance of £1,240 at 30 April 20X9. Upon comparison with the bank statement, you determine that there are unpresented cheques totalling £450, and a receipt of £140 which has not yet been passed through the bank account. The bank statement shows bank charges of £75 which have not been entered in the cash book.

The balance on the bank statement is

A £1,005 overdrawn

B £930 overdrawn

C £1,475

D £1,550

8   Which of the following is NOT a valid reason for the cash book and bank statement failing to agree?

A Timing difference

B Bank charges

C Error

D Cash receipts posted to creditors

9   The bank statement at 31 December 20X1 shows a balance of £1,000. The cash book shows a balance of £750 in hand. Which of the following is the most likely reason for the difference.

A Receipts of £250 recorded in cash book, but not yet recorded by bank

B Bank charges of £250 shown on the bank statement, not in the cash book

C Standing orders of £250 included on bank statement, not in the cash book

D Cheques for £250 recorded in the cash book, but not yet gone through the bank account

10   The cash book balance at 30 November 20X2 shows an overdraft of £500. Cheques for £6,000 have been written and sent out, but do not yet appear on the bank statement. Receipts of £5,000 are in the cash book, but are not yet on the bank statement. What is the balance on the bank statement?

A £1,500

B £500 in hand

C £1,500 in hand

D £500 overdrawn

7   CONTROL ACCOUNTS

1   You are given the following information:

Debtors at 1 January 20X3	£10,000
Debtors at 31 December 20X3	£9,000
Total receipts during 20X3 (including cash sales of £5,000)	£85,000

Sales on credit during 20X3 amount to

A   £81,000
B   £86,000
C   £79,000
D   £84,000

2   A supplier sends you a statement showing a balance outstanding of £14,350. Your own records show a balance outstanding of £14,500.

The reason for this difference could be that

A   The supplier sent an invoice for £150 which you have not yet received

B   The supplier has allowed you £150 cash discount which you had omitted to enter in your ledgers

C   You have paid the supplier £150 which he has not yet accounted for

D   You have returned goods worth £150 which the supplier has not yet accounted for

3   The sales ledger control account at 1 May had balances of £32,750 debit and £1,275 credit. During May, sales of £125,000 were made on credit. Receipts from debtors amounted to £122,500 and cash discounts of £550 were allowed. Refunds of £1,300 were made to customers. The closing balances at 31 May could be

A   £35,175 debit and £3,000 credit
B   £35,675 debit and £2,500 credit
C   £36,725 debit and £2,000 credit
D   £36,725 debit and £1,000 credit

4   The debit side of a trial balance totals £50 more than the credit side. This could be due to

A   A purchase of goods for £50 being omitted from the creditor's account
B   A sale of goods for £50 being omitted from the debtor's account
C   An invoice of £25 for electricity being credited to the electricity account
D   A receipt for £50 from a debtor being omitted from the cash book

5   A sales ledger control account had a closing balance of £8,500. It contained a contra to the purchase ledger of £400, but this had been entered on the wrong side of the control account.

The correct balance on the control account should be

A   £7,700 debit
B   £8,100 debit
C   £8,400 debit
D   £8,900 debit

6   A trader who is not registered for VAT purposes buys goods on credit. These goods have a list price of £2,000, exclusive of VAT, and the trader is given a trade discount of 20%. The goods carry VAT at 17.5%.

The correct ledger entries to record this purchase are to debit the purchases account and to credit the supplier's account with

A   £1,600
B   £1,880
C   £2,000
D   £2,350

7   Your purchase ledger control account has a balance at 1 October 20X8 of £34,500 credit. During October, credit purchases were £78,400, cash purchases were £2,400 and payments made to suppliers, excluding cash purchases, and after deducting cash discounts of £1,200, were £68,900. Purchase returns were £4,700.

The closing balance was:

A   £38,100
B   £40,500
C   £47,500
D   £49,900

8   The sales account is

A   Credited with the total of sales made, including VAT
B   Credited with the total of sales made, excluding VAT
C   Debited with the total of sales made, including VAT
D   Debited with the total of sales made, excluding VAT

9   At the end of the month, an organisation needs to accrue for one week's wages. The gross wages amount to £500, tax amounts to £100, employer's national insurance is £50, employees' national insurance is £40, and employees' contributions to pension scheme amount to £30. The ledger entries to record this accrual would be

A	Debit wages expense	£500	Credit national insurance creditor	£90
			Credit income tax creditor	£100
			Credit pension scheme creditor	£30
			Credit wages accrued	£280
B	Debit wages expense	£550	Credit national insurance creditor	£90
			Credit income tax creditor	£100
			Credit pension scheme creditor	£30
			Credit wages accrued	£330
C	Debit wages expense	£280	Credit wages accrued	£500
	Debit national insurance expense	£90		
	Debit income tax expense	£100		
	Debit pension scheme expense	£30		
D	Debit wages expense	£330	Credit wages accrued	£550
	Debit national insurance expense	£90		
	Debit income tax expense	£100		
	Debit pension scheme expense	£30		

10   If sales (including VAT) amounted to £27,612.50, and purchases (excluding VAT) amounted to £18,000, the balance on the VAT account, assuming all items are subject to VAT at 17.5%, would be

    A   £962.50 debit

    B   £962.50 credit

    C   £1,682.10 debit

    D   £1,682.10 credit

8   ERRORS AND SUSPENSE ACCOUNTS I

1   Splodge plc's accounts contain two errors. A £10,000 bad debt written off has been deducted from sales and a £20,000 credit note received has been added to sales. Before correction, turnover was £1m and cost of sales was £800,000. What is the gross profit margin after correction of these errors?

    A   17.8%

    B   18.8%

    C   21.2%

    D   22.2%

2   After calculating your company's profit for 20X3, you discover that:

    (a)   A fixed asset costing £50,000 has been included in the purchases account;

    (b)   Stationery costing £10,000 has been included as closing stock of raw materials, instead of stock of stationery.

    These two errors have had the effect of

    A   Understating gross profit by £40,000 and understating net profit by £50,000

    B   Understating both gross profit and net profit by £40,000

    C   Understating gross profit by £60,000 and understating net profit by £50,000

    D   Overstating both gross profit and net profit by £60,000

3   The suspense account shows a debit balance of £100. This could be due to

    A   Entering £50 received from A Turner on the debit side of A Turner's account

    B   Entering £50 received from A Turner on the credit side of A Turner's account

    C   Undercasting the sales day book by £100

    D   Undercasting the purchases account by £100

4   The capital of a sole trader would change as a result of

    A   A creditor being paid his account by cheque

    B   Raw materials being purchased on credit

    C   Fixed assets being purchased on credit

    D   Wages being paid in cash

5   You are the accountant of ABC Ltd and have extracted a trial balance at 31 October 20X4. The sum of the debit column of the trial balance exceeds the sum of the credit column by £829. A suspense account has been opened to record the difference. After preliminary investigations failed to locate any errors, you have decided to prepare draft final accounts in accordance with the prudence concept.

The suspense account balance would be treated as

A   An expense in the profit and loss account
B   Additional income in the profit and loss account
C   An asset in the balance sheet
D   A liability in the balance sheet

6   Where a transaction is credited to the correct ledger account, but debited incorrectly to the repairs and renewals account instead of to the plant and machinery account, the error is known as an error of

A   Omission
B   Commission
C   Principle
D   Original entry

7   If a purchase return of £48 has been wrongly posted to the debit of the sales returns account, but has been correctly entered in the supplier's account, the total of the trial balance would show

A   The credit side to be £48 more than the debit side
B   The debit side to be £48 more than the credit side
C   The credit side to be £96 more than the debit side
D   The debit side to be £96 more than the credit side

8   A suspense account shows a credit balance of £130. This could be due to

A   Omitting a sale of £130 from the sales ledger

B   Recording a purchase of £130 twice in the purchases account

C   Failing to write off a bad debt of £130

D   Recording an electricity bill paid of £65 by debiting the bank account and crediting the electricity account.

9   An organisation restores its petty cash balance to £500 at the end of each month. During January, the total column in the petty cash book was recorded as being £420, and hence the imprest was restored by this amount. The analysis columns, which had been posted to the nominal ledger, totalled only £400. This error would result in

A   No imbalance in the trial balance
B   The trial balance being £20 higher on the debit side
C   The trial balance being £20 higher on the credit side
D   The petty cash balance being £20 lower than it should be

10   An invoice from a supplier of office equipment has been debited to the stationery account. This error is known as

A   An error of commission
B   An error of original entry
C   A compensating error
D   An error of principle

9 ERRORS AND SUSPENSE ACCOUNTS II

1 An error of principle would occur if

A Plant and machinery purchased was credited to a fixed assets account

B Plant and machinery purchased was debited to the purchases account

C Plant and machinery purchased was debited to the equipment account

D Plant and machinery purchased was debited to the correct account but with the wrong amount

2 An organisation's year end is 30 September. On 1 January 20X6 the organisation took out a loan of £100,000 with annual interest of 12%. The interest is payable in equal instalments on the first day of April, July, October and January in arrears.

How much should be charged to the profit and loss account for the year ended 30 September 20X6, and how much should be accrued on the balance sheet?

	Profit and loss account	*Balance sheet*
A	£12,000	£3,000
B	£9,000	£3,000
C	£9,000	nil
D	£6,000	£3,000

3 A suspense account was opened when a trial balance failed to agree. The following errors were later discovered.

- A gas bill of £420 had been recorded in the gas account as £240

- A discount of £50 given to a customer had been credited to discounts received

- Interest received of £70 had been entered in the bank account only

The original balance on the suspense account was

A Debit £210
B Credit £210
C Debit £160
D Credit £160

4 An error of commission is one where

A A transaction has not been recorded

B One side of a transaction has been recorded in the wrong class of account, such as fixed assets posted to stock

C An error has been made in posting a transaction

D The digits in a number are recorded the wrong way round

5 Where a transaction is entered into the correct ledger accounts, but the wrong amount is used, the error is known as an error of

A Omission
B Original entry
C Commission
D Principle

6   A business's bank balance increased by £750,000 during its last financial year. During the same period it issued shares of £1 million and repaid a debenture of £750,000. It purchased fixed assets for £200,000 and charged depreciation of £100,000. Working capital (other than the bank balance) increased by £575,000.

Its profit for the year was

A   £1,175,000
B   £1,275,000
C   £1,325,000
D   £1,375,000

7   A sole trader's business made a profit of £32,500 during the year ended 31 March 20X8. This figure was after deducting £100 per week wages for himself. In addition, he put his home telephone bill through the business books, amounting to £400 plus VAT at 17.5%. He is registered for VAT and therefore has charged only the net amount to his profit and loss account.

His capital at 1 April 20X7 was £6,500. His capital at 31 March 20X8 was

A   £33,730
B   £33,800
C   £38,930
D   £39,000

8   Which ONE of the following is an error of principle?

A   A gas bill credited to the gas account and debited to the bank account

B   The purchase of a fixed asset credited to the asset account at cost and debited to the creditor's account

C   The purchase of a fixed asset debited to the purchases account and credited to the creditor's account

D   The payment of wages debited and credited to the correct accounts, but using the wrong amount

9   A business can make a profit and yet have a reduction in its bank balance. Which ONE of the following might cause this to happen?

A   The sales of fixed assets at a loss
B   The charging of depreciation in the profit and loss account
C   The lengthening of the period of credit given to customers
D   The lengthening of the period of credit taken from suppliers

10   The purpose of charging depreciation on fixed assets is to

A   Put money aside to replace the assets when required
B   Show the assets in the balance sheet at their current market value
C   Ensure that the profit is not understated
D   Spread the net cost of the assets over their estimated useful life

10   FINAL ACCOUNTS AND AUDIT I

1   Hengist, a sole trader, has calculated that his cost of sales for the year is £144,000. His sales figure for the year includes an amount of £2,016 being the amount paid by Hengist himself into the business bank account for goods withdrawn for private use. The figure of £2,016 was calculated by adding a mark-up of 12% to the cost of the goods. His gross profit percentage on all other goods sold was 20%.

What is the total sales figure for the year?

A   £172,656
B   £177,750
C   £179,766
D   £180,000

2   The bookkeeper of Leggit Ltd has disappeared. There is no cash in the till and theft is suspected. It is known that the cash balance at the beginning of the year was £240. Since then, total sales have amounted to £41,250. Credit customers owed £2,100 at the beginning of the year and owe £875 now. Cheques banked from credit customers have totalled £24,290. Expenses paid from the till receipts amount to £1,850 and cash receipts of £9,300 have been lodged in the bank.

How much has the bookkeeper stolen during the period?

A   £7,275
B   £9,125
C   £12,155
D   £16,575

3   A club takes credit for subscriptions when they become due. On 1 January 20X5 arrears of subscriptions amounted to £38 and subscriptions paid in advance were £72. On 31 December 20X5 the amounts were £48 and £80 respectively. Subscription receipts during the year were £790.

In the income and expenditure account for 20X5 the income from subscriptions would be shown as:

A   £748
B   £788
C   £790
D   £792

4   A club takes no credit for subscriptions due until they are received. On 1 January 20X5 arrears of subscriptions amounted to £24 and subscriptions paid in advance were £14. On 31 December 20X5 the amounts were £42 and £58 respectively. Subscription receipts during the year were £1,024.

In the income and expenditure account for 20X5 the income from subscriptions would be shown as:

A   £956
B   £980
C   £998
D   £1,050

5   For many years, life membership of the Tipton Poetry Association cost £100, but with effect from 1 January 20X5 the rate has been increased to £120. The balance on the life membership fund at 31 December 20X4 was £3,780 and membership details at that date were as follows:

	No of members
Joined more than 19 years ago	32
Joined within the last 19 years	64
	96

The Association's accounting policy is to release life subscriptions to income over a period of 20 years beginning with the year of enrolment.

During 20X5, four new members were enrolled and one other member (who had joined in 20X1) died.

What is the balance on the life membership fund at 31 December 20X5?

A   £3,591

B   £3,841

C   £3,916

D   £4,047

6   In the operating profit note of a cashflow statement it is usual to find adjustments for items not involving cash movement. Which one of the following items might appear under such a heading?

A   The profit on disposal of fixed assets

B   The accumulated depreciation on fixed assets

C   The profit and loss account charge for taxation

D   The provision for doubtful debts

7   A company has an authorised share capital of 1,000,000 ordinary shares of £1 each, of which 800,000 have been issued at a premium of 50p each, thereby raising capital of £1,200,000. The directors are considering allocating £120,000 for dividend payments this year.

This amounts to a dividend of

A   12p per share

B   10p per share

C   15p per share

D   12%

8   Your company sells goods on 29 December 20X3, on sale or return; the final date for return or payment in full is 10 January 20X4. The costs of manufacturing the product are all incurred and paid for in 20X3 except for an outstanding bill for carriage outwards which is still unpaid.

The associated revenues and expenses of the transaction should be dealt with in the profit and loss account by

A   Including all revenues and all expenses in 20X3

B   Including all revenues and all expenses in 20X4

C   Including expenses in 20X3 and revenues in 20X4

D   Including the revenue and the carriage outwards in 20X4, and the other expenses in 20X3

9   Which one of the following would you expect to find in the appropriation account of a limited company, for the current year?

    A   Preference dividend proposed during the previous year, but paid in the current year
    B   Preference dividend proposed during the current year, but paid in the following year
    C   Directors' fees
    D   Auditors' fees

10   The following information relates to a company at its year end.

	£
Stock at beginning of year	
Raw materials	10,000
Work-in-progress	2,000
Finished goods	34,000
Stock at end of year	
Raw materials	11,000
Work-in-progress	4,000
Finished goods	30,000
Purchases of raw materials	50,000
Direct wages	40,000
Royalties on goods sold	3,000
Production overheads	60,000
Distribution costs	55,000
Administration expenses	70,000
Sales	300,000

The cost of goods manufactured during the year is

    A   £147,000
    B   £151,000
    C   £153,000
    D   £154,000

11   FINAL ACCOUNTS AND AUDIT II

1   In a not-for-profit organisation, the accumulated fund is

    A   Long-term liabilities plus current liabilities plus current assets
    B   Fixed assets less current liabilities less long-term liabilities
    C   The balance on the general reserves account
    D   Fixed assets plus net current assets less long-term liabilities

2   A 'true and fair view' is one which

    A   Presents the accounts in such a way as to exclude errors which would affect the actions of those reading them

    B   Occurs when the accounts have been audited

    C   Shows the accounts of an organisation in an understandable format

    D   Shows the assets on the balance sheet at their current market price

3   A business commenced with a bank balance of £3,250; it subsequently purchased goods on credit for £10,000; gross profit mark-up was 120%; half the goods were sold for cash, less cash discount of 5%; all takings were banked.

The resulting net profit was

A   £700
B   £3,700
C   £5,450
D   £5,700

4   An income and expenditure account is

A   A summary of the cash and bank transactions for a period

B   Another name for a receipts and payments account

C   Similar to a profit and loss account in reflecting revenue earned and expenses incurred during a period

D   A balance sheet as prepared for a non-profit making organisation

5   Revenue reserves are

A   Accumulated and undistributed profits of a company
B   Amounts which cannot be distributed as dividends
C   Amounts set aside out of profits to replace revenue items
D   Amounts set aside out of profits for a specific purpose

6   A company has £100,000 of ordinary shares at a par value of 10 pence each and 100,000 5% preference shares at a par value of 50 pence each. The directors decide to declare a dividend of 5p per ordinary share.

The total amount (ignoring tax) to be paid out in dividends amounts to

A   £5,000
B   £7,500
C   £52,500
D   £55,000

7   The correct ledger entries needed to record the issue of 200,000 £1 shares at a premium of 30p, and paid for by cheque, in full, would be

A	DEBIT	share capital account	£200,000
	CREDIT	share premium account	£60,000
	CREDIT	bank account	£140,000
B	DEBIT	bank account	£260,000
	CREDIT	share capital account	£200,000
	CREDIT	share premium account	£60,000
C	DEBIT	share capital account	£200,000
	CREDIT	share premium account	£60,000
	CREDIT	bank account	£260,000
D	DEBIT	bank account	£200,000
	DEBIT	share premium account	£60,000
	CREDIT	share capital account	£260,000

8   If work-in-progress decreases during the period, then

   A   Prime cost will decrease
   B   Prime cost will increase
   C   The factory cost of goods completed will decrease
   D   The factory cost of goods completed will increase

9   An organisation's cash book has an opening balance in the bank column of £485 credit. The following transactions then took place.

   (i)   Cash sales £1,450 including VAT of £150
   (ii)   Receipts from customers of debts of £2,400
   (iii) Payments to creditors of debts of £1,800 less 5% cash discount
   (iv)   Dishonoured cheques from customers amounting to £250

   The resulting balance in the bank column of the cash book should be

   A   £1,255 debit
   B   £1,405 debit
   C   £1,905 credit
   D   £2,375 credit

10   A club received subscriptions during 20X5 totalling £12,500. Of these, £800 related to 20X4 and £400 related to 20X6. There were subscriptions in arrears at the end of 20X5 of £250. The subscriptions to be included in the income and expenditure account for 20X5 amount to

   A   £11,050
   B   £11,550
   C   £11,850
   D   £12,350

12   FINAL ACCOUNTS AND AUDIT III

1   A manufacturer has the following figures for the year ended 30 September 20X6:

Direct materials	£8,000
Factory overheads	£12,000
Direct labour	£10,000
Increase in work-in-progress	£4,000

   Prime cost is

   A   £18,000
   B   £26,000
   C   £30,000
   D   £34,000

2   An increase in the figure for work-in-progress will

   A   Increase the prime cost
   B   Decrease the prime cost
   C   Increase the cost of goods sold
   D   Decrease the factory cost of goods completed

3   Life membership fees payable to a club are usually dealt with by

A   Crediting the total received to a life membership fees account and transferring a proportion each year to the income and expenditure account

B   Crediting the total received to the income and expenditure account in the year in which these fees are received

C   Debiting the total received to a life membership fees account and transferring a proportion each year to the income and expenditure account

D   Debiting the total received to the income and expenditure account in the year in which these fees are received

4   A company has authorised capital of 50,000 5% preference shares of £2 each and 500,000 ordinary shares with a par value of 20p each. All of the preference shares have been issued, and 400,000 ordinary shares have been issued at a premium of 30p each. Interim dividends of 5p per ordinary share plus half the preference dividend have been paid during the current year. A final dividend of 15p per ordinary share is declared.

The total of dividends payable for the year is

A   £82,500
B   £85,000
C   £102,500
D   £105,000

5   Your company auditor insists that it is necessary to record items of plant separately and to depreciate them over several years, but that items of office equipment, such as hand-held stapling machines, can be grouped together and written off against profits immediately.

The main reason for this difference in treatment between the two items is because

A   Treatment of the two items must be consistent with treatment in previous periods

B   Items of plant last for several years, whereas hand-held stapling machines last only for months

C   Hand-held stapling machines are not regarded as material items

D   Items of plant are revalued from time to time, whereas hand-held stapling machines are recorded at historical cost

6   The main purpose of an audit is to

A   Detect errors and fraud

B   Ensure that the accounts are accurate

C   Determine that the accounts show a true and fair view of the financial state of the organisation

D   Carry out compliance tests on the internal control system

7   You are given the following information for the year ended 31 October 20X7:

	£
Purchases of raw materials	112,000
Returns inwards	8,000
Decrease in stocks of raw materials	8,000
Direct wages	42,000
Carriage outwards	4,000
Carriage inwards	3,000
Production overheads	27,000
Increase in work-in-progress	10,000

The value of factory cost of goods completed is

A   £174,000
B   £182,000
C   £183,000
D   £202,000

8   The responsibility for ensuring that all accounting transactions are properly recorded and summarised in the final accounts lies with

A   The external auditors
B   The internal auditors
C   The shareholders
D   The directors

9   A club's membership fees account shows a debit balance of £150 and a credit balance of £90 at 1 June 20X7. During the year ending 31 May 20X8, subscriptions received amounted to £4,750. Subscriptions overdue from the year ended 31 May 20X7, of £40, are to be written off. At 31 May 20X8, subscriptions paid in advance amount to £75.

The amount to be transferred to the income and expenditure account for the year ending 31 May 20X8 is

A   £4,575
B   £4,655
C   £4,775
D   £4,875

10   The record of how the profit or loss of a company has been allocated to distributions and reserves is found in the

A   Capital account
B   Profit and loss account
C   Reserves account
D   Appropriation account

13   FINAL ACCOUNTS AND AUDIT IV

1   Revenue reserves would decrease if a company

A   Sets aside profits to pay future dividends
B   Transfers amounts into 'general reserves'
C   Issues shares at a premium
D   Pays dividends

2   A receipts and payments account is similar to:

    A   An income and expenditure account

    B   A profit and loss account

    C   A trading account

    D   A cash book summary

3   Your firm has the following manufacturing figures.

	£
Prime cost	56,000
Factory overheads	4,500
Opening work in progress	6,200
Factory cost of goods completed	57,000

    Closing work-in-progress is

    A   £700

    B   £2,700

    C   £9,700

    D   £11,700

4   A major aim of the internal auditors is to

    A   Reduce the costs of the external auditors by carrying out some of their duties

    B   Support the work of the external auditors

    C   Prepare the financial accounts

    D   Report to shareholders on the accuracy of the accounts

5   The subscriptions receivable account of a club commenced the year with subscriptions in arrears of £50 and subscriptions in advance of £75. During the year, £12,450 was received in subscriptions, including all of the arrears and £120 for next year's subscriptions

    The amount to be taken to the income and expenditure account for the year is

    A   £12,205

    B   £12,355

    C   £12,545

    D   £12,595

6   The prime cost of goods manufactured is the total of

    A   All factory costs before adjusting for work-in progress

    B   All factory costs of goods completed

    C   All materials and labour

    D   Direct factory costs

7   Ensuring that the assets of a company are properly safeguarded and utilised efficiently and effectively is part of

    A   The stewardship function exercised by the directors

    B   The external auditor's responsibility

    C   The function of the financial accountant

    D   The internal auditor's responsibility

8   Which ONE of the following does NOT form part of the equity capital of a limited company?

    A   Preference share capital
    B   Share premium
    C   Revaluation reserve
    D   Ordinary share capital

9   A true and fair view is given by the accounts when:

    A   Assets are stated at their true values in the balance sheet

    B   They have been audited and found to be accurate

    C   They fairly reflect the financial position of an organisation, sufficient for users of the accounts to make proper judgements

    D   The auditors are able to certify that they contain no errors or omissions, and that no fraud has been committed

10   A sole trader has net assets of £19,000 at 30 April 20X0. During the year to 30 April 20X0, he introduced £9,800 additional capital into the business. Profits were £8,000, of which he withdrew £4,200. His capital at 1 May 20W9 was:

    A   £3,000
    B   £5,400
    C   £13,000
    D   £16,600

14   INTERPRETATION OF ACCOUNTS

1   Horsa's sales follow a seasonal pattern. Monthly sales in the final quarter of the year are twice as high as during other periods. He also benefits from a higher mark-up during the final quarter: an average of 25% on cost compared with 20% during the rest of the year.

Horsa's sales in 20X9 totalled £210,000. What was the amount of his gross profit?

    A   £36,750
    B   £37,800
    C   £39,667
    D   £46,200

2   Which one of the following formulae should be used to calculate the rate of stock turnover in a retail business?

    A   Sales divided by average stock
    B   Sales divided by year-end stock
    C   Purchases divided by year-end stock
    D   Cost of sales divided by average stock

3   A company's working capital was £43,200. Subsequently, the following transactions occurred.

(a)   Creditors were paid £3,000 by cheque.
(b)   A bad debt of £250 was written off.
(c)   Stock valued at £100 was sold for £230 on credit.

Working capital is now

A   £43,080
B   £46,080
C   £40,080
D   £42,850

4   The formula for calculating the rate of stock turnover is

A   Average stock at cost divided by cost of goods sold
B   Sales divided by average stock at cost
C   Sales divided by average stock at selling price
D   Cost of goods sold divided by average stock at cost

5   Given a selling price of £350 and a gross profit mark-up of 40%, the cost price would be

A   £100
B   £140
C   £210
D   £250

6   Which of the following transactions would result in an increase in capital employed?

A   Selling stocks at a profit
B   Writing off a bad debt
C   Paying a creditor in cash
D   Increasing the bank overdraft to purchase a fixed asset

7   Sales are £110,000. Purchases are £80,000. Opening stock is £12,000. Closing stock is £10,000.

The rate of stock turnover is

A   7.27 times
B   7.45 times
C   8 times
D   10 times

8   The rate of stock turnover is 6 times where

A   Sales are £120,000 and average stock at selling price is £20,000
B   Purchases are £240,000 and average stock at cost is £40,000
C   Cost of goods sold is £180,000 and average stock at cost is £30,000
D   Net purchases are £90,000 and closing stock at cost is £15,000

9   Working capital will reduce by £500 if

A   Goods costing £3,000 are sold for £3,500 on credit
B   Goods costing £3,000 are sold for £3,500 cash
C   Fixed assets costing £500 are purchased on credit
D   Fixed assets with a net book value of £750 are sold for £250 cash

10   From the following information regarding the year to 31 August 20X6, what is the creditors' payment period?

	£
Sales	43,000
Cost of sales	32,500
Opening stock	6,000
Closing stock	3,800
Creditors at 31 August 20X6	4,750

A   40 days
B   50 days
C   53 days
D   57 days

15   RATIOS

1   A business operates on a gross profit margin of $33^1/_3$%. Gross profit on a sale was £800, and expenses were £680.

The net profit percentage is

A   3.75%
B   5%
C   11.25%
D   22.67%

2   During the year ended 31 October 20X7, your organisation made a gross profit of £60,000, which represented a mark-up of 50%. Opening stock was £12,000 and closing stock was £18,000.

The rate of stock turnover was

A   4 times
B   6.7 times
C   7.3 times
D   8 times

3   A business has the following trading account for the year ending 31 May 20X8:

	£	£
Sales turnover		45,000
Opening stock	4,000	
Purchases	26,500	
	30,500	
Less: closing stock	6,000	
		24,500
Gross profit		20,500

Its rate of stock turnover for the year is

A   4.9 times
B   5.3 times
C   7.5 times
D   9 times

4   A company's gearing ratio would rise if

 A A decrease in long-term loans is *less* than a decrease in shareholders' funds
 B A decrease in long-term loan is *more* than a decrease in shareholders' funds
 C Interest rates rose
 D Dividends were paid

5   A company has the following details extracted from its balance sheet:

	£'000
Stocks	1,900
Debtors	1,000
Bank overdraft	100
Creditors	1,000

Its liquidity position could be said to be

 A Very well-controlled because its current assets far outweigh its current liabilities

 B Poorly-controlled because its quick assets are less than its current liabilities

 C Poorly-controlled because its current ratio is significantly higher than the industry norm of 1.8

 D Poorly-controlled because it has a bank overdraft

6   The gross profit mark-up is 40% where

 A Sales are £120,000 and gross profit is £48,000
 B Sales are £120,000 and cost of sales is £72,000
 C Sales are £100,800 and cost of sales is £72,000
 D Sales are £100,800 and cost of sales is £60,480

7   A company has the following current assets and liabilities at 31 October 20X8:

		£'000
Current assets:	stock	970
	debtors	380
	bank	40
		1,390
Current liabilities	creditors	420

When measured against accepted 'norms', the company can be said to have:

 A a high current ratio and an ideal acid test ratio
 B an ideal current ratio and a low acid test ratio
 C a high current ratio and a low acid test ratio
 D ideal current and acid test ratios

8   Your company's profit and loss account for the year ended 30 September 20X8 showed the following:

	£'000
Net profit before interest and tax	1,200
Interest	200
	1,000
Corporation tax	400
Retained profit for the year	600

Its balance sheet at 30 September 20X7 showed the following capital:

	£'000
Share capital	8,000
Profit and loss account balance	1,200
	9,200
10% debenture	2,000
	11,200

Return on average capital employed for the year ended 30 September 20X8 is

A   5.88%

B   10.17%

C   10.43%

D   none of these

9   An increase in both debtors' and creditors' payment periods could result in:

A   An increase in working capital

B   A decrease in working capital

C   An increase in current assets and current liabilities

D   A decrease in current assets and current liabilities

10   The gearing ratio is often calculated as

A   Long-term loans and current liabilities as a percentage of total shareholders' funds

B   Current and long-term debt as a percentage of total net assets

C   Long-term loans and preference shares as a percentage of total shareholders' funds

D   Preference shares as a percentage of equity capital

Objective test questions

CONCEPTUAL AND REGULATORY FRAMEWORK

16

It has been suggested that there are seven separate user groups of published accounting statements. These include owner/investors, loan creditors, analysts/advisors, business contacts, for example, customers and suppliers and the public. Which two are missing?

1. ▬▬▬▬▬▬▬▬▬▬▬▬▬

2. ▬▬▬▬▬▬▬▬▬▬▬▬▬

17

Dee has given you a piece of paper with two statements about accounting concepts.

(a) A business continues in existence for the foreseeable future.

(b) Revenues and expenses should be recognised in the period in which they are earned or incurred.

Required

Name the two accounting concepts described above.

1. ▬▬▬▬▬▬▬▬▬▬▬▬▬

2. ▬▬▬▬▬▬▬▬▬▬▬▬▬

18

The following statement describes an accounting concept. 'In conditions of uncertainty more confirmatory evidence is required about the existence of an asset or a gain than about the existence of a liability or a loss.'

Which accounting concept is being described here? ▬▬▬▬▬▬▬▬▬▬

19

A business has incurred the following expenses. You are to complete the table indicating whether the expenditure is capital expenditure or revenue expenditure.

	Capital expenditure	*Revenue expenditure*
Redecoration of factory		
New engine for machinery		
Cleaning of factory		
Purchase of delivery van		

20

Closing stocks are deducted from purchases and opening stocks in the profit and loss account in order to determine the cost of sales. Of which accounting concept is this an example? ▬▬▬▬▬▬▬▬▬▬▬▬▬

21

Accounting standards are issued by the Financial Reporting Council.

True or False?

LEDGER ACCOUNTING AND BOOKS OF PRIME ENTRY

22

Your organisation sold goods to PQ Limited for £800 less trade discount of 20% and cash discount of 5% for payment within 14 days. The invoice was settled by cheque five days later. What is the double entry for the cash discount allowed?

Debit £	*Credit* £
▓▓▓▓▓▓▓▓▓▓▓▓▓▓▓▓	
	▓▓▓▓▓▓▓▓▓▓▓▓▓▓▓▓

23

The following totals appear in the day books for March 20X8.

	Goods excluding VAT £	*VAT* £
Sales day book	40,000	7,000
Purchases day book	20,000	3,500
Returns inwards day book	2,000	350
Returns outward day book	4,000	700

Opening and closing stocks are both £3,000.

The gross profit for March 20X8 is ▓▓▓▓▓▓▓▓▓.

24

Diesel fuel in stock at 1 November 20X7 was £12,500, and there were invoices awaited for £1,700. During the year to 31 October 20X8, diesel fuel bills of £85,400 were paid, and a delivery worth £1,300 had yet to be invoiced. At 31 October 20X8, the stock of diesel fuel was valued at £9,800.

The diesel fuel to be charged to the profit and loss account for the year to 31 October 20X8 is ▓▓▓▓▓▓▓▓▓.

25

An increase in the provision for doubtful debts results in a decrease in ▓▓▓▓▓▓▓▓▓▓▓ and increases/decreases the profit for the year (circle as appropriate).

26

The petty cash imprest is restored to £100 at the end of each week. The following amounts are paid out of petty cash during week 23.

Stationery	£14.10 including VAT at 17.5%
Travelling costs	£25.50
Office refreshments	£12.90
Sundry creditors	£24.00 plus VAT at 17.5%

The amount required to restore the imprest to £100 is ▓▓▓▓▓▓▓▓▓ .

27

A company's telephone bill consists of two elements. One is a quarterly rental charge, payable in advance; the other is a quarterly charge for calls made, payable in arrears. At 1 April 20X9, the previous bill dated 1 March 20X9 had included line rental of £90. Estimated call charges during March 20X9 were £80.

During the following 12 months, bills totalling £2,145 were received on 1 June, 1 September, 1 December 20X9 and 1 March 20Y0, each containing rental of £90 as well as call charges. Estimated call charges for March 20Y0 were £120.

The amount to be charged to the profit and loss account for the year ended 31 March 20Y0 is ▓▓▓▓▓▓▓▓ .

The following data relates to questions 28-31

At 1 October 20X5, the following balances were brought forward in the ledger accounts of XY:

Rent payable account	Dr	£1,000
Electricity account	Cr	£800
Interest receivable account	Dr	£300
Provision for doubtful debts account	Cr	£4,800

You are told the following.

(a)   Rent is payable quarterly in advance on the last day of November, February, May and August, at the rate of £6,000 per annum.

(b)   Electricity is paid as follows.

5 November 20X5	£1,000 (for the period to 31 October 20X5)
10 February 20X6	£1,300 (for the period to 31 January 20X6)
8 May 20X6	£1,500 (for the period to 30 April 20X6)
7 August 20X6	£1,100 (for the period to 31 July 20X6)

At 30 September 20X6, the electricity meter shows that £900 has been consumed since the last bill was received.

(c)   Interest was received during the year as follows.

2 October 20X5	£250 (for the six months to 30 September 20X5)
3 April 20X6	£600 (for the six months to 31 March 20X6)

You estimate that interest of £300 is accrued at 30 September 20X6.

(d)   At 30 September 20X6, the balance of debtors amounts to £125,000. The provision for doubtful debts is to be amended to 5% of debtors.

28

The rent charge to the profit and loss account for the year is £ ▓▓▓▓▓▓▓

29

The charge for electricity to the profit and loss account for the year is £ ▓▓▓▓▓▓

30

The amount of interest receivable to appear in the profit and loss account for the year is £ ▓▓▓▓▓

31

The charge or credit to the profit and loss account for doubtful debts is £▓▓▓▓▓▓

Charge/credit (circle as appropriate)

The following data relates to questions 32 to 37

Your organisation has recently employed a new accounts assistant who is unsure about the correct use of books of original entry and the need for adjustments to be made to the accounts at the end of the year. You have been asked to give the new assistant some guidance.

For each of the following examples of transactions to be recorded in the books of original entry complete the double entry posting sheet below.

32

Purchase of raw materials on credit from J Burgess, list price £27,000 less trade discount of 33 1/3 %, plus VAT of 17.5%.

33

Payment to a creditor, P Barton, by cheque in respect of a debt of £14,000, less cash discount of 2%.

34

Receipt of a piece of office equipment in payment of a debt of £2,500 from a debtor, J Smithers.

35

Write off a debt of £500 due from A Scholes.

36

Returns of goods sold to J Lockley, total invoice value of £470, including VAT of 17.5%.

37

Purchase of a motor vehicle on credit from A Jackson, for £1,400, including road fund (vehicle licence) tax of £75.

DOUBLE ENTRY POSTING SHEET

ITEM	BOOK OF ORIGINAL ENTRY	DEBIT ENTRIES		CREDIT ENTRIES	
		Account	£	Account	£
(i)					
(ii)					
(iii)					
(iv)					
(v)					
(vi)					

The following data relates to questions 38 to 39

Business rates are paid annually on 1 April, to cover the following 12 months. The business rates for 20X1/X2 are £1,800, and for 20X2/20X3 are increased by 20%. Rent is paid quarterly on the first day of May, August, November and February, in arrears. The rent has been £1,200 per annum for some time, but increases to £1,600 per annum from 1 February 20X2.

38

The charge for business rates in the profit and loss account for the year ended 30 April 20X2 is £

39

The charge for rent in the profit and loss account for the year ended 30 April 20X2 is £

STOCKS

40

SSAP 9 recognises two main ways of calculating cost of stocks. What are they? Complete the blanks below

1.

2.

The following data relates to questions 41 to 43

The trading account of T Ltd is set out below:

T Ltd

Trading Account for the year ended 30 April 20X1

	£'000	£'000
Turnover		1,000
Opening stock	200	
Purchases	700	
	900	
Closing stock	300	
Cost of goods sold		600
Gross profit		400

The opening and closing stock in T Ltd was valued on a FIFO basis. On a LIFO basis the opening and closing stock would have been valued at £180,000 and £270,000 respectively.

41

     The gross profit if LIFO had been used for stock valuation would have been £ ▨

42

     What are the 'stock days', using average stock during the year, on the assumption that stock is valued on the FIFO basis?

43

     What are the 'stock days', using the average method, on the assumption that stock is valued on the LIFO basis?

FIXED ASSETS

44

A machine cost £9,000. It has an expected useful life of six years, and an expected residual value of £1,000. It is to be depreciated at 30% per annum on the reducing balance basis. A full year's depreciation is charged in the year of purchase, with none in the year of sale. During year 4, it is sold for £3,000.

The profit or loss on disposal is ▨▨▨▨▨▨▨▨.

45

The accounting concept which dictates that fixed assets should be valued at cost, less accumulated depreciation, rather than their enforced saleable value, is the ▨▨▨▨▨▨▨▨ concept.

46

A fixed asset was disposed of for £2,200 during the last accounting year. It had been purchased exactly three years earlier for £5,000, with an expected residual value of £500, and had been depreciated on the reducing balance basis, at 20% per annum.

The profit or loss on disposal was ▨▨▨▨▨▨▨.

47

By charging depreciation in the accounts, a business aims to ensure that the cost of fixed assets is spread ▨▨▨▨▨▨▨▨▨▨ which benefit from their use.

48

A machine was purchased in 20X6 for £64,000. It was expected to last for 5 years and to have a residual value of £2,000. Depreciation was charged at 50% per annum on the reducing balance method, with a full year's charge in the year of purchase. No depreciation is charged in the year of disposal. The company's year end is 31 December. The machine was sold on 3 April 20Y0 for £5,500. The profit or loss on sale is ▨▨▨▨▨▨▨▨.

The following data relates to questions 49 and 50

On 1 January 20X1 a business purchased a laser printer costing £1,800. The printer has an estimated life of 4 years after which it will have no residual value.

49

Calculate the depreciation charge for 20X2 on the laser printer on the straight line basis:

▨▨▨▨▨▨▨▨▨▨▨▨▨▨▨
▨▨▨▨▨▨▨▨▨▨▨▨▨▨▨

BPP
PROFESSIONAL EDUCATION

50

Calculate the depreciation charge for 20X2 on the laser printer on the reducing balance basis at 60% per annum

BANK RECONCILIATIONS

The following data relates to questions 51 and 52

On 10 January 20X9, Jane Smith received her monthly bank statement for December 20X8. The statement showed the following.

SOUTHERN BANK PLC

J Smith: Statement of Account

Date	Particulars	Debits	Credits	Balance
20X8		£	£	£
Dec 1	Balance			1,862
Dec 5	417864	243		1,619
Dec 5	Dividend		26	1,645
Dec 5	Bank Giro Credit		212	1,857
Dec 8	417866	174		1,683
Dec 10	417867	17		1,666
Dec 11	Sundry Credit		185	1,851
Dec 14	Standing Order	32		1,819
Dec 20	417865	307		1,512
Dec 20	Bank Giro Credit		118	1,630
Dec 21	417868	95		1,535
Dec 21	417870	161		1,374
Dec 24	Bank charges	18		1,356
Dec 27	Bank Giro Credit		47	1,403
Dec 28	Direct Debit	88		1,315
Dec 29	417873	12		1,303
Dec 29	Bank Giro Credit		279	1,582
Dec 31	417871	25		1,557

Her cash book for the corresponding period showed:

CASH BOOK

20X8		£	20X8		Cheque no	£
Dec 1	Balance b/d	1,862	Dec 1	Electricity	864	243
Dec 4	J Shannon	212	Dec 2	P Simpson	865	307
Dec 9	M Lipton	185	Dec 5	D Underhill	866	174
Dec 19	G Hurst	118	Dec 6	A Young	867	17
Dec 26	M Evans	47	Dec 10	T Unwin	868	95
Dec 27	J Smith	279	Dec 14	B Oliver	869	71
Dec 29	V Owen	98	Dec 16	Rent	870	161
Dec 30	K Walters	134	Dec 20	M Peters	871	25
			Dec 21	L Philips	872	37
			Dec 22	W Hamilton	873	12
			Dec 31	Balance c/d		1,793
		2,935				2,935

51

Calculate the corrected cash book balance as at 31 December 20X8:

52

Fill in the missing words and figures.

To reconcile the balance per the bank statement at 31 December 20X8 with the corrected cashbook balance at that date:

- Add _____ of £ _____ ; and

- Deduct _____ of £ _____ .

The following data relates to question 53

Sandilands Ltd uses a computer package to maintain its accounting records. A printout of its cash book for the month of May 20X3 was extracted on 31 May and is summarised below.

	£		£
Opening balance	546	Payments	335,966
Receipts	336,293	Closing balance	873
	336,839		336,839

The company's chief accountant provides you with the following information.

(a) The company's bank statement for May was received on 1 June and showed an overdrawn balance of £1,444 at the end of May.

(b) Cheques paid to various creditors totalling £7,470 have not yet been presented to the bank.

(c) Cheques received by Sandilands Ltd totalling £6,816 were paid into the bank on 31 May but not credited by the bank until 2 June.

(d) Bank charges of £630 shown on the bank statement have not been entered in the company's cash book.

(e) Standing orders entered on the bank statement totalling £2,584 have not been recorded in the company's cash book.

(f) A cheque drawn by Sandilands Ltd for £693 and presented to the bank on 26 May has been incorrectly entered in the cash book as £936.

53

The corrected cash book balance at 31 May is £ _____

54

At 31 December 20X9 the cash book of a company shows a credit balance of £901. When the bank statement for the month of December was compared with the cash book, it was discovered that cheques totalling £2,468 had been drawn but not presented to the bank, and cheques received totalling £593 had not yet been credited by the bank.

The balance on the bank statement at 31 December 20X9 was _____

CONTROL ACCOUNTS

55

An employee is paid at the rate of £3.50 per hour. Earnings of more than £75 a week are taxed at 20%. Employees' National Insurance is 7%, and Employer's National Insurance is 10%. During week 24, the employee works for 36 hours.

The amounts to be charged to the profit and loss account and paid to the employee are:

Profit and loss account	*Paid to employee*

56

A sales ledger control account showed a debit balance of £37,642. The individual debtors' accounts in the sales ledger showed a total of £35,840. The difference could be due to entering cash discount allowed of ▨ on the debit side of the control account.

57

A business paid out £12,450 in net wages to its employees. In respect of these wages, the following amounts were shown in the balance sheet.

	£
Income tax creditor	2,480
National Insurance creditor – employees'	1,350
– employer's	1,500
Pension creditor for employees' contributions	900

Employees' gross wages, before deductions, were ▨.

58

A debit balance of £1,250 on X's account in the books of Y means that:

X ▨ Y

59

A business has the following transactions for the month of June 20X2:

Credit sales (including VAT at 17.5%)	164,500
Sales returns (including VAT at 17.5%)	6,200
Cheques from debtors	155,300
Discounts allowed to customers	5,100
Bad debts written off	2,600

The debtors balance at 30 June 20X2 was £8,300.

The debtors balance at 1 June 20X2 was £ ▨

60

The following totals have been extracted from the books of a business at 30 September 20X2.

	£
Sales day book total	367,520
Purchases day book total	227,540
Returns inwards day book total	13,445
Returns outwards day book total	9,045
Discounts allowed	5,220
Discounts received	2,070
Cash receipts from debtors	361,200
Cash payments to creditors	210,040

The purchase ledger control account had a balance of £17,600 at 1 September 20X2. During the month a journal entry has recorded a contra entry between a debtors account and a creditors account of £940.

The balance on the purchase ledger control account at 30 September 20X2 is £ �░░░░░░

CORRECTION OF ERRORS AND SUSPENSE ACCOUNTS

61   An organisation restores its petty cash balance to £250 at the end of each month. During October, the total expenditure column in the petty cash book was calculated as being £210, and the imprest was restored by this amount. The analysis columns posted to the nominal ledger totalled only £200.

This error would result in the trial balance being £10 higher on the ░░░░░░░░ side.

62

A trial balance has an excess of debits over credits of £14,000 and a suspense account has been opened to make it balance. It is later discovered that:

(a)   The discounts allowed balance of £3,000 and the discounts received balance of £7,000 have both been entered on the wrong side of the trial balance.

(b)   The creditors control account balance of £233,786 had been included in the trial balance as £237,386.

(c)   An item of £500 had been omitted from the sales records (ie from the sales day book).

(d)   The balance on the current account with the senior partner's wife had been omitted from the trial balance. This item when corrected removes the suspense account altogether.

The balance on the current account with the senior partner's wife is £ ░░░░░░░░░

The following data relates to questions 63 to 71

After calculating net profit for the year ended 31 March 20X8, WL has the following trial balance.

	DR £	CR £
Land and buildings – cost	10,000	
Land and buildings - depreciation at 31 March 20X8		2,000
Plant – cost	12,000	
Plant - depreciation at 31 March 20X8		3,000
Stocks	2,500	
Debtors	1,500	
Bank	8,250	
Creditors		1,700
Rent prepaid	400	
Wages accrued		300
Capital account		19,400
Profit for the year ended 31 March 20X8		9,750
	34,650	36,150

A suspense account was opened for the difference in the trial balance.

Immediately after production of the above, the following errors were discovered:

(i)   A creditor's account had been debited with a £300 sales invoice (which had been correctly recorded in the sales account).

(ii)   The heat and light account had been credited with gas paid £150.

(iii)   G Gordon had been credited with a cheque received from G Goldman for £800. Both are debtors.

(iv)   The insurance account contained a credit entry for insurance prepaid of £500, but the balance had not been carried down and hence had been omitted from the above trial balance.

(v)   Purchase returns had been over-cast by £700 when posting to the purchases returns account.

63

Prepare a journal entry to correct error (i).

	DR £	CR £

64

Prepare a journal entry to correct error (ii).

	DR £	CR £

65

Prepare a journal entry to correct error (iii).

	DR £	CR £
	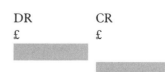	

66

Prepare a journal entry to correct error (iv).

	DR £	CR £

67

Prepare a journal entry to correct error (v).

	DR £	CR £

68

The net profit for the year after correction of errors (i) to (v) is £

69

The figure for debtors in the amended balance sheet is £

70

The figure for prepayments in the amended balance sheet is £

71

The figure for creditors in the amended balance sheet is £

FINAL ACCOUNTS AND AUDIT

The following data relates to questions 72 to 74

The following trial balance has been extracted from the ledger of Mr Yousef, a sole trader.

TRIAL BALANCE AS AT 31 MAY 20X6

	Dr £	Cr £
Sales		138,078
Purchases	82,350	
Carriage	5,144	
Drawings	7,800	
Rent, rates and insurance	6,622	
Postage and stationery	3,001	
Advertising	1,330	
Salaries and wages	26,420	
Bad debts	877	
Provision for doubtful debts		130
Debtors	12,120	
Creditors		6,471
Cash in hand	177	
Cash at bank	1,002	
Stock as at 1 June 20X5	11,927	
Equipment		
At cost	58,000	
Accumulated depreciation		19,000
Capital		53,091
	216,770	216,770

The following additional information as at 31 May 20X6 is available.

(a)   Rent is accrued by £210.
(b)   Rates have been prepaid by £880.
(c)   £2,211 of carriage represents carriage inwards on purchases.
(d)   Equipment is to be depreciated at 15% per annum using the straight line method.
(e)   The provision for bad debts is to be increased by £40.
(f)   Stock at the close of business has been valued at £13,551.

72

     The gross profit for the year is £ ▨

73

     The rent, rates and insurance charge for the year is £ ▨

74

     Fill in the figures.

     Summarised balance sheet at 31 May 20X6

	£	£
Fixed assets		▨
Current assets	▨	
Less: Current liabilities	▨	
Net current assets		▨
Total assets less current liabilities		▨

75

At 1 November 20X8, a club's membership subscriptions account show a debit balance of £200 and a credit balance of £90. During the year ended 31 October 20X9, subscriptions received amounted to £4,800. At 31 October 20X9, subscriptions paid in advance amounted to £85 and subscriptions in arrears (expected to be collected) to £50.

The amount to be transferred to the income and expenditure account in respect of subscriptions for the year ended 31 October 20X9 is ░░░░░░░░░░░░░░░░░░░.

76

The *accumulated fund* represents ░░.

The following data relates to questions 77 to 82

Miss Anne Teek runs a market stall selling old pictures, china, copper goods and curios of all descriptions. Most of her sales are for cash although regular customers are allowed credit. No double entry accounting records have been kept, but the following information is available.

SUMMARY OF NET ASSETS AT 31 MARCH 20X8

	£	£
Motor van		
Cost	3,000	
Depreciation	2,500	
Net book value		500
Current assets		
Stock	500	
Debtors	170	
Cash at bank	2,800	
Cash in hand	55	
	3,525	
Less current liabilities		
Creditors	230	
Net current assets		3,295
		3,795

Additional information

(a) Anne bought a new motor van in January 20X9 receiving a part exchange allowance of £1,800 for her old van. A full year's depreciation is to be provided on the new van, calculated at 20% on cost.

(b) Anne has taken £50 cash per week for her personal use. She also estimates that petrol for the van, paid in cash, averages £10 per week.

(c) Other items paid in cash were as follows.

Sundry expenses   £24
Repairs to stall canopy   £201

(d) Anne makes a gross profit of 40% on selling prices. She is certain that no goods have been stolen but remembers that she appropriated a set of glasses and some china for her own use. These items had a total selling price of £300.

(e) Trade debtors and creditors at 31 March 20X9 are £320 and £233 respectively, and cash in hand amounts to £39. No stock count has been made and there are no accrued or prepaid expenses.

Objective test questions

A summary of bank statements for the twelve months in question shows the following.

Credits	£
Cash banked (all cash sales)	7,521
Cheques banked (all credit sales)	1,500
Dividend income	210
	9,231

Debits	£
Purchase of motor van	3,200
Road fund licence	80
Insurance on van	323
Creditors for purchases	7,777
Rent	970
Sundry	31
Accountancy fees (re current work)	75
Bank overdraft interest (six months to 1 October 20X8)	20
Returned cheque (bad debt)	29
	12,505

The bank statement for 1 April 20X9 shows an interest charge of £27.

Assume a 52 week year.

77

The cash sales for the year were £

78

The credit sales for the year were £

79

The purchases for the year to be included in the trading account were £

80

The van depreciation charge for the year was £

81

The profit or loss on disposal of the old van was £

82

The van depreciation charge and the profit or loss on disposal of the old van must be taken into account in arriving at the net profit or loss for the year. What is the **total** of the **other expenses** that are deducted from gross profit to give the net profit for the year ended 31 March 20X9?

83

Opening stock is £1,000, purchases are £10,000 and sales are £15,000. The gross profit margin is 30%. Closing stock is £ .

84

The following information is for the year ended 31 October 20X0.

	£
Purchases of raw materials	56,000
Returns inwards	4,000
Increase in stock of raw materials	1,700
Direct wages	21,000
Carriage inwards	2,500
Production overheads	14,000
Decrease in work-in-progress	5,000

The value of factory cost of goods completed is ▨.

The following data relates to questions 85 and 86

Balances at 31 December 20X4

	£
Fixed assets (cost £60,000)	39,000
Stocks	
Raw materials	25,000
Work in progress, valued at prime cost	5,800
Finished goods	51,000

The following relevant transactions occurred during 20X5.

Invoiced purchases of raw materials, less returns	80,000
Discounts received	1,700
Factory wages paid	34,000
Manufacturing expenses paid	61,900

Balances at 31 December 20X5

	£
Fixed assets (cost £90,000)	60,000
Stocks	
Raw materials	24,000
Work in progress	5,000
Finished goods	52,000

85

The prime cost of production for the year was £ ▨

86

The total depreciation charge for the year was £ ▨

87

At the beginning of the year in GHI Ltd, the opening work in progress was £240,000. During the year the following expenditure was incurred:

	£
Prime cost	720,000
Factory overheads	72,000

The closing work in progress was £350,000.

The factory cost of goods completed during the year was £ ▭

88

At the start of the year a manufacturing company had stocks of raw materials of £18,000 and stocks of finished goods of £34,000. There was no work in progress.

During the year the following expenses were incurred:

	£
Raw materials purchased	163,000
Manufacturing expenses incurred	115,000

During the year sales of £365,000 were made. The stocks of raw materials at the year end were valued at £21,000 and the stocks of finished goods were valued at £38,000. There was no work in progress.

The gross profit for the year is £ ▭

89

A company made a profit for the year of £18,750, after accounting for depreciation of £1,250. During the year, fixed assets were purchased for £8,000, debtors increased by £1,000, stock decreased by £1,800 and creditors increased by £350.

The increase in cash and bank balances during the year was ▭.

INTERPRETATION OF ACCOUNTS

The following data relates to questions 90 and 91

KK Ltd has made a profit before tax of £445,000. There is to be a provision for corporation tax for the year of £111,000, a transfer to general reserve of £30,000 and a proposed final dividend of £60,000. During the year an interim dividend of £40,000 was paid. Trade creditors and accruals totalled £17,000.

90

The retained profit for the year was £ ▭

91

The total creditors to be shown in the balance sheet were £ ▭

The following data relates to questions 92 and 93

Given below are extracts from the trial balance of FG Ltd at 31 March 20X2 after preparation of the draft profit and loss account.

	£
Share capital (50 pence ordinary shares)	200,000
Share premium account	40,000
General reserve	20,000
Profit and loss account reserve at 31 March 20X2	84,000

Since preparation of the draft profit and loss account it has been discovered that three items had not been accounted for.

(i)   On 1 April 20X1 the company issued 100,000 new ordinary shares at a price of 80 pence per share.

(ii)   Closing stock had been over stated by £10,000.

(iii)   The directors wished to make a transfer to the general reserve of £5,000.

92

The amended balance on the profit and loss account reserve at 31 March 20X2 was
£ ▓▓▓▓▓▓▓▓

93

Fill in the figures below.

	£
Share capital	▓▓▓▓▓▓▓
Share premium	▓▓▓▓▓▓▓
General reserve	▓▓▓▓▓▓▓

94

A company had the following gross profit calculation in its last accounting period.

	£
Sales	130,000
Cost of sales	60,000
Gross profit	70,000

Average stock during that period was £7,500.

In the next accounting period sales are expected to increase by 40%, and the rate of stock turnover is expected to double. If average stock remains at £7,500 the gross profit mark-up percentage will be ▓▓▓▓▓ %.

95

The gross profit mark-up is ▓▓▓▓▓ % where sales are £240,000 and cost of sales is £150,000.

The following data relates to questions 96 and 97

7 mins

The following figures have been extracted from the published accounts of MBC plc, at 31 October 20X5.

	£m
Ordinary share capital	30
Share premium	3
Reserves	5
	38
6% debentures	10
	48

The net profit (after tax of £1m) for the year to 31 October 20X5 was £4m and dividends amounted to £0.5m.

96

Calculate the company's gearing ratio.

97

Calculate the company's return on average capital employed (ROCE).

The following data relates to questions 98 to 104

ARH plc has the following results for the last two years of trading.

ARH PLC
TRADING AND PROFIT AND LOSS ACCOUNT FOR THE YEAR ENDED

	31.12.X4	31.12.X5
	£'000	£'000
Sales	14,400	17,000
Less cost of sales	11,800	12,600
Gross profit	2,600	4,400
Less expenses	1,000	2,000
Less interest	200	-
Net profit for the year	1,400	2,400
Dividends proposed	520	780
Retained profit for the year	880	1,620

ARH PLC
BALANCE SHEET

	31 December 20X4		*31 December 20X5*	
	£'000	£'000	£'000	£'000
Fixed assts		2,500		4,000
Current assets				
Stocks	1,300		2,000	
Debtors	2,000		1,600	
Bank balances	2,400		820	
	5,700		4,420	
Less current liabilities				
Creditors	1,500		2,700	
Net current assets		4,200		1,720
		6,700		5,720
Less long term liabilities				
10% debentures		2,600		-
		4,100		5,720
Financed by:				
2.4 million ordinary shares of £1 each		2,400		2,400
Revaluation reserves		500		500
Retained profits		1,200		2,820
		4,100		5,720

98

The gross profit margin is

	20X4	20X5
	%	%

99

The net profit margin is

	20X4	20X5
	%	%

100

The return on capital employed is

	20X4	20X5

101

The acid test ratio is

	20X4	20X5

102

The asset turnover is

	20X4	20X5

BPP
PROFESSIONAL EDUCATION

103

The stock turnover period in days is

	20X4 Days	20X5 Days

104

The gearing ratio is

	20X4 %	20X5 %

Answers

Answers to multiple choice questions

1   CONCEPTUAL AND REGULATORY FRAMEWORK

1   A   Fails to take account of changing price levels over time.

2   B   Remember you were asked for the *main* aim.

3   D   Current purchasing power accounting.

4   C   Overstating profits and understating balance sheet asset values.

5   C   Assets less liabilities = opening capital plus profits less drawings.

∴ Assets less liabilities less opening capital plus drawings = profit

6   D   Separate entity concept. A business is separate from its owner.

7   D   Improvements are capital expenditure, repairs and maintenance are not.

8   A   Accruals concept.

9   D   Once capital has been maintained, anything earned in excess is profit.

10   B   This is just a rewording of question 4, be careful with these in the exam.

2   DOUBLE ENTRY BOOKKEEPING I

1   D   Gross profit – expenses = net profit.

2   C   Prepayment b/f £900 (9/12 × £1,200) + £1,600 – prepayment c/f £1,200 (9/12 × £1,600).

3   D   A decrease in the provision is written back to profit.

4   B   Accruals. The stationery must be charged to the period in which it was consumed.

5   A   Y is a creditor of X.

6   C   Trade discounts are not included in the cost of purchases.

7   C   Sales less returns inwards. Discounts allowed are shown as a deduction from gross profit.

8   D

CREDITORS CONTROL ACCOUNT

	£		£
Bank	542,300	Balance b/d	142,600
Discounts	13,200	∴ Purchases	578,200
Returns	27,500		
Balance c/d	137,800		
	720,800		720,800

9   D   £10,200 + £3,000 + £1,400 = £14,600.

10   C

	£
Opening stock	165
Purchases (1,350 – 80 + 70)	1,340
	1,505
Closing stock	140
Stationery in P&L	1,365

3   DOUBLE ENTRY BOOKKEEPING II

1   A   Decrease = £400 + £1,200 – £250.

2   D   A liability or a revenue.

3   C   The sales ledger.

4   C   Ledger accounts are posted from books of prime entry.

5   D

	£
Opening stock	12,000
Purchases (bal. fig)	122,000
Purchase returns	(5,000)
Closing stock	(18,000)
Cost of goods sold	111,000

6   C   Check against question 2 above.

7   D

	£
Assets	
Opening cash	1,000
Cash received £(1,000 + 175 VAT)	1,175
Closing cash	2,175
Stock £(800-400)	400
	2,575
Liabilities	
Opening liabilities	-
VAT creditor	175
Purchase stock	800
Closing liabilities	975
Capital	
Opening capital	1,000
Profit on sale of stock £(1,000 – 400)	600
Closing capital	1,600

8   B

	£
Opening capital	10,000
Capital introduced	4,000
Drawings	(8,000)
Loss (bal.fig)	(1,500)
Closing capital	4,500

9   D   As X is a creditor, only a return of goods would generate a credit entry.

10   A

MOTOR EXPENSES

	£			£
1.9 Prepayment b/d	80	1.9	Accrual b/d	95
Cash	95	30.9	Prepayment (80 × 3/4)	60
Cash	245		P&L c/d	385
30.9 Accrual c/d	120			
	540			540

4   STOCKS

1   B   FIFO will treat stock on hand as the most recent purchases, which are the most expensive.

2   C   Cost of sales is £1,300 understated and expenses £1,000 understated.

3   C   Closing stock = 20 units @ £3 each = £60

4   D   2 @ £3.00 + 10 @ £3.50 = £41.00

5   C

	Units	Unit cost £	Total £	Average £
Opening stock	30	2	60	
5 August purchase	50	2.40	120	
	80		180	2.25
10 August issue	(40)	2.25	(90)	
	40		90	
18 August purchase	60	2.50	150	
	100		240	2.40
23 August issue	(25)	2.40	(60)	
	75		180	

6   B

		£	£
Sales			148,000
COS	Opening stock	34,000	
	Purchases	100,000	
		134,000	
	Closing stock (bal fig)	(26,000)	
			108,000
			40,000

7   C

	Quantity	Value £	
1 October (60 × £12)	60	720	
8 October (40 × £15)	100	1,320	
14 October (50 × £18)	150	2,220	(ie average cost £14.80)
21 October (75 × £14.80)	75	1,110	

8   B

Stock card	£	No	£	Average
6 @ £15	90	6	90	
10 @ £19.80	198	16	288	18.00
10 @ £18	(180)	6	108	18.00
20 @ £24.50	490	26	598	23.00
5 @ £23	(115)	21	483	

	£
Sales (15 @ £30)	450
Issues (10 @ £18 + 5 @ £23)	(295)
Profit	155

9   A   FIFO values stock at the latest prices.

10   C   SSAP 9 specifically discourages the use of LIFO and replacement costs.

5   FIXED ASSETS

1   A   It is **never** B as funds are not set aside; nor C, this is revaluation.

2   D   (£5,000 – £1,000)/4 = £1,000 depreciation per annum ∴ NBV = £2,000.

3   D

	£
Balance b/d	67,460
Less NBV of fixed asset sold	
15,000 – (15,000 – (4,000 + 1,250))	5,250
	62,210

4   A   If disposal proceeds were £15,000 and profit on disposal is £5,000, then net book value must be £10,000, the difference between the fixed asset register figure and the fixed asset account in the nominal ledger.

5   A   The stationery would appear as an asset rather than as an expense

6   C   Compare this with the answers to 1 above

7   C

	£
Profit	8,000
Add back: depreciation	12,000
Net cash inflow	20,000
Purchase of fixed assets for cash	(25,000)
Decrease in cash	5,000

8   A   We would need to know *either* sale proceeds *or* length of time in order to calculate the other.

9   A

Ledger accounts

	£
As at 1.1.X7	
Cost	60,000
Depreciation	15,000
	45,000

Fixed asset register

	£
At 1.1.X7	
Net book value	47,500
Disposal of asset which cost £(4,000 + 1,500)	(5,500)
	42,000

10   B

		£
Year 1	Purchase	2,400.00
Year 1	Depreciation	(480.00)
		1,920.00
Year 2	Depreciation	(384.00)
		1,536.00
Year 3	Depreciation	(307.20)
		1,228.80
Year 4	Sale proceeds	1,200.00
	Loss on disposal	(28.80)

6   BANK RECONCILIATIONS

1   B   £(565)o/d – £92 dishonoured cheque = £(657) o/d

2   D   The question refers to the figure to be shown in the balance sheet.

	£	£
Balance per cash book		5,675
Reversal – Standing order entered twice	125	
Adjustment – Dishonoured cheque (450 × 2) entered in error as a debit		900
Bank overdraft	6,450	
	6,575	6,575

3   A

	£	£
Opening bank balance	2,500	
Payment (£1,000 – £200) × 90%		720
Receipt (£200 – £10)	190	
Closing bank balance		1,970
	2,690	2,690

4   B

	£	£
Balance per bank statement		800
Unpresented cheque		80
Dishonoured cheque ★		–
Corrected balance	880	
	880	880

★ This has already been deducted from the balance on the bank statement.

5   B

	£
Cash book balance	2,490
Adjustment re charges	(50)
Adjustment re dishonoured cheque	(140)
	2,300

6   B

	£	£
Bank statement balance b/d	13,400	
Dishonoured cheque	300	
Bank charges not in cash book	50	
Unpresented cheques		2,400
Uncleared bankings	1,000	
Adjustment re error (2 × 195)		390
Cash book balance c/d		11,960
	14,750	14,750
Cash book balance b/d	11,960	

Alternative approach:

	£	£
Cash book balance b/d	11,960	
Dishonoured cheque		300
Bank charges not in cash book		50
Unpresented cheques	2,400	
Uncleared bankings		1,000
Adjustment re error (2 × 195)	390	
Bank statement balance c/d		13,400
	14,750	14,750
Bank statement balance b/d	13,400	

7   A

	£	£
Cash book (the cash book has a credit balance)		1,240
Unpresented cheques	450	
Uncleared deposit		140
Bank charges		75
Bank overdraft	1,005	
	1,455	1,455

8   D   Provided that the cash receipts have been correctly posted to the cash book, then the fact that they have incorrectly been posted to creditors instead of cash sales or debtors will not affect the bank reconciliation.

9   D   All the other options would have the bank account £250 less than the cash book.

10   B

	£	£
Cash book		500
Unpresented cheques	6,000	
Uncleared deposit		5,000
Bank balance		500
	6,000	6,000

7   CONTROL ACCOUNTS

1   C   Credit sales = £80,000 – £10,000 + £9,000 = £79,000.

2   B   All of the other options would lead to a *higher* balance in the supplier's records

3   C   Debits total £32,750 + £125,000 + £1,300 = £159,050. Credits total £1,275 + £122,550 + £550 = £124,325. ∴ Net balance = £34,725 debit.

4   A   The other options would make the credit side total £50 more than the debit side.

5   A   £8,500 – (2 × £400) = £7,700.

6   B   The trader cannot recover the VAT so it is included in purchases

	£
List price	2,000
Trade discount: 20%	400
	1,600
VAT at 17½%	280
	1,880

7   A

	£
Opening balance	34,500
Credit purchases	78,400
Discounts	(1,200)
Payments	(68,900)
Purchase returns	(4,700)
	38,100

8   B   The VAT element of the invoices will go to the VAT account in the balance sheet.

9   B   The cost to the business consists of gross wage plus employer's NI.

10   B

	£
Output VAT £27,612.50 $\times \dfrac{17.5}{117.5}$	4,112.50
Input VAT £18,000 $\times \dfrac{17.5}{100}$	3,150.00
∴ Balance on VAT a/c (credit)	962.50

8   ERRORS AND SUSPENSE ACCOUNTS I

1   C

	£'000
Turnover (£1m + £10,000 – £20,000)	990
Cost of sales (£800,000 – £20,000)	780
Gross profit	210

Gross profit margin $= \dfrac{210}{990} \times 100 = 21.2\%$

2   A   Both errors will affect cost of sales and therefore gross profit, making a net effect of £40,000. Net profit will be further reduced by £10,000 missing from stationery stocks.

3   D   A and B will only affect the personal ledgers, C will cause an incorrect double entry.

4   D   In the other three cases only balance sheet accounts are affected and there is an equal and opposite debit and credit.

5   D   Remember these are **draft** accounts. No suspense account should remain in the final accounts.

6   C   An error of principle.

7   D   Debits will exceed credits by 2 × £48 = £96

8   B   A would give a debit balance of £130, C would have no effect and D would not cause a trial balance imbalance.

9   C   Think of the double entry. Bank has been credited by £420 but expenses only debited by £400.

10   D   An error of principle.

9   ERRORS AND SUSPENSE ACCOUNTS II

1   B   A and C are errors of commission, D is an error of original entry.

2   B   £9,000 is payable (P&L), but only £6,000 paid (April and July).

3   A

SUSPENSE ACCOUNT

	£		£
Balance b/d	210	Gas bill (420 − 240)	180
Interest	70	Discount (2 × 500)	100
	280		280

4   C   A is an error of omission, B is an error of principle, D is a transposition error.

5   B   The posting is correct, but the wrong amount has been used.

6   A

	£'000
Profit for the year	1,175
Add back depreciation	100
	1,275
Add: Issue of shares	1,000
Less: Repayment of debentures	(750)
Less: Purchase of fixed assets	(200)
	1,325
Less: Increase in working capital	(575)
Increase in bank balance	750

7   C

	£
Capital at 1.4.X7	6,500
Add: Profit (after drawings)	32,500
Less: VAT element	(70)
Capital at 31.3.X8	38,930

8   C   This is a posting made to the wrong class of account.

9   C   This will increase debtors but reduce cash.

10   D   Spread the net cost of the assets over their estimated useful life.

10   FINAL ACCOUNTS AND AUDIT I

1   C

	Total	Ordinary sales	Private drawings
	£	£	£
Cost of sales	144,000	142,200	1,800
Mark-up:			
12% on cost	216	-	216
20% on sales (= 25% on cost)	35,550	35,550	
Sales	179,766	177,750	2,016

2   A   We need to calculate credit sales first in order to calculate cash sales.

DEBTORS

	£		£
Bal b/f	2,100	Bank	24,290
∴ Credit sales	23,065	Bal c/f	875
	25,165		25,165

CASH

	£		£
Balance b/f	240	Expenses	1,850
Cash sales		Bank	9,300
(41,250 – 23,065)	18,185	∴ Theft	7,275
	18,425		18,425

3   D

	£	£
Subscriptions received in 20X5		790
Less: amounts relating to 20X4	38	
amounts relating to 20X6	80	
		118
Cash received relating to 20X5		672
Add: subs paid in 20X4 relating to 20X5	72	
20X5 subs still to be paid	48	
		120
		792

Alternatively, in ledger account format:

SUBSCRIPTIONS

	£		£
Balance b/f	38	Balance b/f	72
∴ Income and expenditure a/c	792	Cash	790
Balance c/f	80	Balance c/f	48
	910		910

4   B

	£
Subscriptions received in 20X5	1,024
Less amounts relating to 20X6	58
	966
Add subs paid in 20X4 relating to 20X5	14
	980

Alternatively, in ledger account format:

SUBSCRIPTIONS

	£		£
∴ Income and expenditure a/c	980	Balance b/f	14
Balance c/f	58	Bank	1,024
	1,038		1,038

5   B

	£	£
Balance at 1 January		3,780
New enrolments		480
		4,260
Less release to income:		
1 × £80	80	
63 × £5	315	
4 × £6	24	
		419
		3,841

6   A   B and D are balance sheet items, C has not been deducted from operating profit.

7   C   (£120,000 ÷ 800,000)

8   B   The revenue cannot be recognised (or not) until 20X4 and the expenses should be in the same period.

9   B   Preference dividend proposed during the current year, but paid in the following year.

10   A

	£	£
Raw materials		
Opening stock	10,000	
Purchases	50,000	
Closing stock	11,000	
Cost of raw materials		49,000
Direct wages		40,000
Prime cost		89,000
Production overheads		60,000
		149,000
Increase in work in progress		
4,000 – 2,000		(2,000)
Cost of goods manufactured		147,000

11   FINAL ACCOUNTS AND AUDIT II

1   D   Accumulated funds = net assets

2   A   A 'true and fair view' should enable users to make decisions based on the accounts.

3   C

	£	£
Sales (10,000 × 220% × 50%)		11,000
Opening stock	-	
Purchases	10,000	
	10,000	
Closing stock	(5,000)	
Cost of goods sold		5,000
Gross profit		6,000
Less discount (5% × 11,000)		550
Net profit		5,450

4   C   It is similar to a profit and loss account and based on the accruals concept.

5   A   Accumulated and undistributed profits of a company

6   C   (£100,000 × 10) × 5p + £50,000 (100,000/50p) × 5% = £50,000 ordinary + £2,500 preference.

7   B   The total will be £260,000, of which £60,000 will be credited to share premium.

8   D   Because some of the WIP has been consumed to complete those goods.

9   B   £(485) o/d + £1,450 + £2,400 – £1,710 (£1,800 × 95%) – £250 = £1,405 debit balance.

10   B

	£
Subscriptions received	12,500
Add subscriptions in arrears c/f	250
	12,750
Deduct: subscriptions in arrears b/f	800
subscriptions in advance c/f	400
	11,550

12   FINAL ACCOUNTS AND AUDIT III

1   A   Prime cost is direct material plus direct labour. There are no *direct* expenses.

2   D   Cross-check this with the answer to 11.8.

3   A   These are funds received in advance so are treated as a liability, which diminishes over time.

4   B

	£
Interim ordinary dividends 5p × 400,000	20,000
Preference dividend (50,000 × £2 × 5%)/2	2,500
Paid to date	22,500
Final ordinary dividend 15p × 400,000	60,000
Preference dividend (must be paid before final ordinary dividend)	2,500
	85,000

5   C   The materiality concept applies here.

6   C   This is the *main* purpose.

7   B

	£
Purchase of raw materials	112,000
Decrease in stock of raw materials	8,000
Carriage inwards	3,000
Raw materials used	123,000
Direct wages	42,000
Prime cost	165,000
Production overheads	27,000
Increase in WIP	(10,000)
Factory cost of finished goods	182,000

8   D   This is part of their stewardship responsibilities.

9   B

SUBSCRIPTIONS ACCOUNT

		£			£
1.6.X7	Balance b/f	150	1.6.X7	Balance b/f	90
31.5.X8	Balance c/f	75		Bank	4,750
31.5.X8	Income and			Bad debts	40
	expenditure a/c	4,655★			
		4,880			4,880

★ ie balancing figure

10   D   Appropriation account

13   FINAL ACCOUNTS AND AUDIT IV

1   D   This is a distribution of reserves.

2   D   It shows receipts and payments and is not based on accruals.

3   C

	£
Prime cost	56,000
Factory overheads	4,500
Opening WIP	6,200
Factory cost of	(57,000)
Therefore closing WIP is	9,700

4   B   The others are not internal audit functions.

5   B

SUBSCRIPTIONS ACCOUNT

	£		£
Balance b/f	50	Balance b/f	75
Balance c/f	120	Bank	12,450
Income and expenditure a/c	12,355		
	12,525		12,525

6   D   Only *direct* costs are included in prime cost.

7   A   The stewardship function exercised by the directors.

8   A   Equity capital is owned by *ordinary* shareholders.

9   C   They give users a 'true and fair' picture of the entity's financial position.

10   B

	£
Opening capital (balancing figure)	5,400
Capital introduced	9,800
Profits	8,000
	23,200
Drawings	(4,200)
	19,000

14   INTERPRETATION OF ACCOUNTS

1   B

	Total	Sales in first three quarters (9/15)	Sales in final quarter (6/15)
	£	£	£
Sales	210,000	126,000	84,000
Mark-up:			
25% on cost (= 20% on sales)	16,800		16,800
20% on cost (=16¹/₂ % on sales)	21,000	21,000	
	37,800		

2   D   Cost of sales tells us what stock has been *used*.

3   A   Transaction (a) would have no effect on working capital.

4   D   You will know this from question 2!

5   D $£350 \times \dfrac{100}{140} = £250$

6   A   Profit will be an addition to owner's capital (accounting equation!)

7   B   Stock turnover $= \dfrac{\text{Cost of sales}}{\text{Average stock}}$

Cost of sales $= 12 + 80 - 10$ $= 82$

Average stock $= \dfrac{12 + 10}{2}$ $= 11$

∴ Stock turnover $= \dfrac{82}{11}$ $= 7.45$ times

8   C   Check this against question 4.

9   C   Fixed assets are not part of working capital but will give rise to a creditor.

10   D   Purchases $= £(32,500 - 6,000 + 3,800)$

$\qquad\qquad\qquad\quad = £30,300$

$\therefore$ Creditors' payment period $= \dfrac{4,750}{30,300} \times 365 = 57$ days

15   RATIOS

1   B

	%	£
Sales	100	2,400
Cost of sales	$66\,^2/_3$	1,600
Gross profit	$33\,^1/_3$	800
Expenses	$28\,^1/_3$	680
Net profit	5	120

2   D

	%	£
Sales	150	180,000
COS	100	(120,000)
Gross profit	50	60,000

$\therefore$ Stock turnover $= \dfrac{120,000}{(12,000 + 18,000)/2} = 8$ times

3   A $\dfrac{\text{Cost of sales}}{\text{Average stock}} = \dfrac{£24,500}{(4,000 + 6,000) \div 2} = 4.9$ times

4   A   Long-term loans raise gearing, shareholders funds reduce it.

5   C   Current ratio is 2,900 : 1,100 = 2.6 : 1 ie high

Acid test ratio is 1,000 : 1,100 = 0.9 ie acceptable

6   C

	£
Sales were	100,800
Cost of sales was	(72,000)
$\therefore$ Gross profit	28,800

Gross profit mark up $= \dfrac{£28,800}{£72,000} \times 100 = 40\%$

7   A   Current ratio $= 1,390:420 \qquad = 3.3:1 \qquad$ (ie high)

Acid test $\quad = 420:420 \qquad\quad = 1:1 \qquad\quad$ (ie ideal)

8   C $\dfrac{\text{PBIT} \times 100}{\text{average capital}} = \dfrac{1,200 \times 100}{(11,200 + 11,800)/2} = 10.43\%$

9   C   Both debtors and creditors will increase.

10   C   Long-term loans and preference shares as a percentage of total shareholders funds.

Answers to objective test questions

CONCEPTUAL AND REGULATORY FRAMEWORK

16

1. Employees

2. The government

17

1. Going concern

2. Accruals

18

Prudence

19

	Capital expenditure	*Revenue expenditure*
Redecoration of factory		★
New engine for machinery	★	
Cleaning of factory		★
Purchase of delivery van	⋏	

20

The accruals concept

21

False. Accounting standards are issued by the Accounting Standards Board.

LEDGER ACCOUNTING AND BOOKS OF PRIME ENTRY

22

	Dr	*Cr*
	£	£
Discount allowed	32	
Debtors control account (PQ Ltd)		32

Sale price £800 – (20% × 800) = £640

Cash discount £640 × 5% = £32

23

The gross profit for March 20X8 is £22,000

Reconstruction of the trading account

	£	£
Sales		40,000
Returns inwards		(2,000)
		38,000
Opening stock	3,000	
Purchases	20,000	
Returns outwards	(4,000)	
Closing stock	(3,000)	
		(16,000)
Gross profit		22,000

24

Diesel fuel charge = £87,700

Diesel fuel creditor account		*Cost of fuel used*	
	£		£
Balance b/fwd	(1,700)	Opening stock	12,500
Payments	85,400	Purchases	85,000
Balance c/fwd	1,300	Closing stock	(9,800)
Purchases	85,000	Transfer to P&L	87,700

25

A decrease in **debtors** and **decreases** the profit for the year.

26

Amounts required to restore imprest = £80.70

	£
Stationery	14.10
Travel	25.50
Refreshments	12.90
Sundry creditors (£24 × 1.175)	28.20
	80.70

27

Telephone charge = £2,185

TELEPHONE ACCOUNT

	£		£
Prepayment b/f (2/3 × £90)	60	Accrual b/f	80
Bills paid	2,145	P&L account	2,185
Accrual c/f	120	Prepayment c/f (2/3 × £90)	60
	2,325		2,325

28

Rent payable = £6,000.

RENT PAYABLE ACCOUNT

		£			£
1.10.X5	Bal b/fwd	1,000	30.9.X6	Charge to P&L a/c	6,000
30.11.X5	Bank	1,500	30.9.X6	Rent prepaid c/fwd	
29.2.X6	Bank	1,500		(1500 × 2/3)	1,000
31.5.X6	Bank	1,500			
31.8.X6	Bank	1,500			
		7,000			7,000
1.10.X6	Rent prepaid b/fwd	1,000			

Alternatively, as you are told that the rent is £6,000 per annum and there has been no increase or decrease this must be the annual charge.

29

Electricity charge = £5,000.

ELECTRICITY ACCOUNT

		£			£
5.11.X5	Bank	1,000	1.10.X5	Bal b/fwd	800
10.2.X6	Bank	1,300	30.9.X6	Charge to P&L a/c	5,000
8.5.X6	Bank	1,500			
7.8.X6	Bank	1,100			
30.9.X6	Accrual c/fwd	900			
		5,800			5,800
			1.10.X6	Balance b/fwd	900

30

Interest receivable = £850.

INTEREST RECEIVABLE ACCOUNT

		£			£
1.10.X5	Bal b/fwd	300	2.10.X5	Bank	250
30.9.X6	Transfer to P&L a/c	850	3.4.X6	Bank	600
			30.9.X6	Accrual c/fwd	300
		1,150			1,150
1.10.X6	Balance b/fwd	300			

31

Provision for doubtful debts = £1,450 charge to profit and loss account.

PROVISION FOR DOUBTFUL DEBTS

		£			£
30.9.X6	Bal c/fwd (125,000 × 5%)	6,250	1.10.X5	Bal b/fwd	4,800
		6,250	30.9.X6	Charge to P&L a/c	1,450
					6,250
			1.10.X6	Balance b/fwd	6,250

32

Book of original entry	Debit entries		Credit entries	
	Account	£	Account	£
Purchase day book	Purchases VAT	18,000 3,150	J Burgess	21,150

33

Book of original entry	Debit entries		Credit entries	
	Account	£	Account	£
Cash book	P Barton	14,000	Bank Discount received	13,720 280

34

Book of original entry	Debit entries		Credit entries	
	Account	£	Account	£
Journal	Office equipment	2,500	J Smithers	2,500

35

Book of original entry	Debit entries		Credit entries	
	Account	£	Account	£
Journal	Bad debts	500	A Scholes	500

36

Book of original entry	Debit entries		Credit entries	
	Account	£	Account	£
Returns inwards day book	Returns inward VAT	400 70	J Lockley	470

37

Book of original entry	Debit entries		Credit entries	
	Account	£	Account	£
Journal	Motor vehicle Motor expenses	1,325 75	A Jackson	1,400

38

Rates payable = £1,830

RATES ACCOUNT

	£		£
1.5.X1 Balance b/f		30.4.X2 Profit and loss a/c	1,830
(1,800 × 11/12)	1,650		
1.4.X2 Rates paid	2,160	30.4.X2 Balance c/f (2,160 × 11/12)	1,980
	3,810		3,810

39

Rent payable = £1,300

RENT ACCOUNT

	£		£
1.5.X1 Rent paid	300	1.5.X1 Balance b/f	300
1.8.X1 Rent paid	300		
1.11.X1 Rent paid	300		
1.2.X2 Rent paid	300		
30.4/X2 Balance c/f (1,600/4)	400	30.4.X2 Profit and loss a/c	1,300
	1,600		1,600

An alternative calculation is:

	£
Rent payable 1.5.X1 to 31.1.X2	
(1,200 × 9/12)	900
Rent payable 1.2.X2 to 30.4.X2	
(1,600 × 3/12)	400
Total rent payable	1,300

STOCKS

40

1. FIFO (first in, first out)

2. Average cost

41

Gross profit: FIFO £400 + adjustment opening stock (£200 - £180) – adjustment closing stock (£270-£300) = £390,000

42

FIFO $\dfrac{(200 + 300)/2}{600} \times 365\,\text{days} = 152\,\text{days}$

43

LIFO $\dfrac{(180 + 270)/2}{610} \times 365\,\text{days} = 135\,\text{days}$

FIXED ASSETS

44

Loss on disposal = £87

	£
$9,000 \times 0.7 \times 0.7 \times 0.7 =$	3,087 (NBV)
Proceeds of sale	(3,000)
Loss on disposal	87

As this is the reducing balance method, the residual value is included in the 30% rate.

45

Going concern concept.

46

Loss on disposal = £360

	£
NBV (£5,000 × 0.8 × 0.8 × 0.8)★	2,560
Proceeds	(2,200)
Loss on disposal	360

★ Remember this is the reducing balance method, the residual value is included in the 20% rate.

47

… over the accounting periods ….

48

Profit on sale = £1,500

	£
NBV (£64,000 × 0.5 × 0.5 × 0.5 × 0.5)	4,000
Proceeds	(5,500)
Profit	1,500

As this is the reducing balance method, the residual value is included in the 50% rate.

49

20X2 depreciation charge = £450

$$\text{Annual depreciation} = \frac{\text{Cost minus residual value}}{\text{Estimated economic life}}$$

$$\text{Annual depreciation} = \frac{£1,800 - £0}{4 \text{ years}}$$

20X2 depreciation = £450

50

20X2 depreciation charge = £432

	£	
Cost at 1.1.20X1	1,800	
Depreciation 20X1	1,080	60% × £1,800
Book value 1.1.20X2	720	
Depreciation 20X2	432	60% × £720
Book value 1.1.20X3	288	

BANK RECONCILIATIONS

51

Corrected cash book balance = £1,681 debit.

CASH BOOK

20X8		£	20X8		£
Dec 31	Balance b/d	1,793	Dec 31	Bank charges	18
Dec 31	Dividend	26	Dec 31	Standing order	32
			Dec 31	Direct debit	88
				Balance c/d	1,681
		1,819			1,819

52

Add **unrecorded lodgements** of £232

Deduct **unpresented cheques** of £108

BANK RECONCILIATION AS AT 31 DECEMBER 20X8

	£	£
Balance per bank statement		1,557
Add unrecorded lodgements:		
V Owen	98	
K Walters	134	
		232
Less unpresented cheques:		
B Oliver (869)	71	
L Philips (872)	37	
		(108)
Balance per cash book (corrected)		1,681

53

Cash book balance = £2,098 overdrawn

CASH BOOK

		£			£
31.5.X3	Balance b/d	873	31.5.X3	Bank charges	630
	Error £(936 - 693)	243		Standing orders	2,584
31.5.X3	Balance c/d	2,098			
		3,214			3,214
			1.6.X3	Balance b/d	2,098

54

Balance per bank statement = £974 (in credit)

BANK RECONCILIATION

	£
Balance per cash book	(901)
Outstanding lodgements	(593)
Unpresented cheques	2,468
Balance per bank statement	974

CONTROL ACCOUNTS

55

	£
36 × £3.50	126.00
Employer's NI	12.60
Gross wages cost (P&L account)	138.60
36 × £3.50	126.00
Tax ((£126 – 75) × 20%)	(10.20)
Employees' NI	(8.82)
Paid to employee	106.98

56

£901

Cash discounts allowed should be credited. So a debit of £901 would result in an error of £1,802 between the ledger and the control account.

57

	£
Wages paid	12,450
Employee deductions – tax	2,480
– NI	1,350
– pension	900
Gross wages	17,180

58

X is a debtor of Y or X owes Y.

59

Balance at 1 June 20X2 = £13,000

DEBTORS CONTROL ACCOUNT

	£		£
Opening balance (bal fig)	13,000	Sales returns	6,200
Sales	164,500	Bank	155,300
		Discounts allowed	5,100
		Bad debts written off	2,600
		Closing balance	8,300
	177,500		177,500

60

Closing balance = £23,045

PURCHASE LEDGER CONTROL ACCOUNT

	£		£
Returns outwards	9,045	Opening balance	17,600
Discounts received	2,070	Purchases	227,540
Bank	210,040		
Contra	940		
Closing balance	23,045		
	245,140		245,140

CORRECTION OF ERRORS AND SUSPENSE ACCOUNTS

61

Credit

The entries are Dr Expenses £200, Cr Bank £210.

62

The balance on the current account is £9,600.

SUSPENSE ACCOUNT

	£		£
		Balance b/d	14,000
Discounts received	14,000	Discounts allowed	6,000
Current a/c – partner's wife	9,600	Creditors control a/c	3,600
	23,600		23,600

63

		£	£
DR	Debtor	300	
CR	Creditor		300

64

		£	£
DR	Heat & light	300	
CR	Suspense account		300

65

		£	£
DR	G Gordon	800	
CR	G Goldman		800

66

		£	£
DR	Insurance prepayment	500	
CR	Suspense account		500

67

		£	£
DR	Purchase returns	700	
CR	Suspense account		700

68

Corrected profit = £8,750

	£
First draft profit	9,750
Adjustment re heat and light	(300)
Adjustment re purchase returns	(700)
Revised net profit	8,750

69

Debtor = £1,800 (£1,500 + £300)

70

Prepayments = £900 (£400 + £500)

71

Creditors = £2,000 (£1,700 + £300)

FINAL ACCOUNTS AND AUDIT

72

Gross Profit = £55,141

	£	£
Sales		138,078
Opening stock	11,927	
Purchases (W)	84,561	
	96,488	
Less closing stock	13,551	
Cost of goods sold		82,937
Gross profit		55,141

Purchases

	£
Per trial balance	82,350
Add carriage inwards	2,211
Per P & L a/c	84,561

73

Rent, rates and insurance = £5,952

	£
Per trial balance	6,622
Add: rent accrual	210
Less: rates prepayment	(880)
	5,952

74

Summarised balance sheet at 31 May 20X6

	£	£
Fixed assets (58,000 − (19,000 + 15% × 58,000))		30,300
Current assets (W)	27,560	
Current liabilities (6,471 + 210)	(6,681)	
Net current assets		20,879
Total assets less current liabilities		51,179

WORKING	£
Stock	13,551
Debtors (12,120 − 130 − 40)	11,950
Prepayment	880
Cash in hand	177
Cash at bank	1,002
	27,560

75

Subscription income = £4,655.

MEMBERSHIP SUBSCRIPTIONS

	£		£
Bal b/f	200	Bal b/f	90
∴ I&E	4,655	Received	4,800
Subs paid in advance c/f	85	Subs in arrears c/f	50
	4,940		4,940

76

The accumulated fund represents the book value of net assets in a not-for-profit organisation.

77

Cash sales = £10,850

CASH BOOK

	Cash £		Cash £
Balance b/d	55	Drawings (52 × £50)	2,600
Cash takings (balancing figure)	10,850	Petrol (52 × £10)	520
		Sundry expenses	24
		Repairs to canopy	201
		Takings banked (contra entry)	7,521
		Balance c/d	39
	10,905		10,905
Balance b/d	39		

78

Credit sales = £1,650.

DEBTORS

	£		£
Balance b/d	170	Cash	1,500
Credit sales - balancing figure	1,650	Balance c/d	320
	1,820		1,820

79

Purchases = £7,600

CREDITORS

	£		£
Bank	7,777	Balance b/d	230
Balance c/d	233	Purchases (balancing figure)	7,780
	8,010		8,010

Goods taken as drawings

		£
Selling price	(100%)	300
Gross profit	(40%)	120
Cost	(60%)	180

Therefore, purchases taken to the trading account = £7,780 – £180 = £7,600.

80

New van depreciation charge = £1,000

The bank statement shows that the cash paid for the new van was £3,200. Since there was a part exchange of £1,800 on the old van, the cost of the new van must be £5,000 with first year depreciation (20%) £1,000.

81

Profit on disposal = £1,300.

	£		£
Van at cost	3,000	Provision for depreciation at	
Profit on disposal	1,300	date of sale	2,500
		Asset account (trade in value for	
		new van)	1,800
	4,300		4,300

82

Other expenses = £2,300

	£	£
Expenses:		
Rent	970	
Repairs to canopy	201	
Van running expenses (520 + 80 + 323)	923	
Sundry expenses (24 + 31)	55	
Bank interest	47	
Accounting fees	75	
Bad debts	29	
		2,300

83

Closing stock = £500.

	£
Sales (100%)	15,000
Gross profit (30%)	4,500
Cost of goods sold (70%)	10,500
Opening stock	1,000
Purchases (from previous question)	10,000
	11,000
Cost of goods sold	10,500
Closing stock (balancing figure)	500

84

Factory cost of goods completed = £96,800.

	£
Purchases of raw materials	56,000
Increase in stocks of raw materials	(1,700)
Direct wages	21,000
Carriage inwards	2,500
Production overheads	14,000
Decrease in work-in-progress	5,000
Factory cost of sales	96,800

Returns inwards are returns of sales and so do not form part of the factory cost of goods.

85

Prime cost = £115,000

	£
Opening stock	25,000
Purchases	80,000
	105,000
Less: closing stock	(24,000)
Raw materials used	81,000
Direct wages	34,000
Prime cost	115,000

86

Total depreciation charge = £9,000

	Fixed assets at cost £	Net book value £	Accumulated depreciation £
At 31 December 20X4	60,000	39,000	21,000
At 31 December 20X5	90,000	60,000	30,000
Depreciation charge for the year		-	9,000

87

The factory cost of goods completed during the year was £682,000

	£
Prime cost	720,000
Factory overheads	72,000
Add: Opening work in progress	240,000
Less: Closing work in progress	(350,000)
Factory cost of goods completed	682,000

88

The gross profit for the year is £94,000

	£
Opening stock of raw materials	18,000
Purchases	163,000
	181,000
Less: closing stock of raw materials	(21,000)
Raw materials used	160,000
Manufacturing expenses	115,000
Factory cost of goods produced	275,000

	£	£
Sales		365,000
Less: Cost of goods sold		
Opening finished goods stock	34,000	
Factory cost of goods produced	275,000	
	309,000	
Less: Closing stock of finished goods	(38,000)	
		271,000
Gross profit		94,000

89

Increase in cash and bank balances = £13,150

	£
Profit for the year	18,750
Add back depreciation	1,250
	20,000
Purchase of fixed assets	(8,000)
Increase in debtors	(1,000)
Decrease in stocks	1,800
Increase in creditors	350
∴ Increase in cash and bank	13,150

INTERPRETATION OF ACCOUNTS

90

Retained profit = £204,000

	£	£
Profit before tax		445,000
Tax		111,000
Profit after tax		334,000
Transfer to general reserve	30,000	
Interim dividend	40,000	
Final proposed dividend	60,000	
		130,000
Retained profit		204,000

91

Total creditors = £188,000

	£
Trade creditors and accruals	17,000
Corporation tax	111,000
Proposed dividend	60,000
	188,000

92

Amended profit and loss reserve = £69,000

	£
Draft profit and loss reserve	84,000
Adjustment for closing stock	(10,000)
Transfer to general reserve	(5,000)
	69,000

93

	£
Share capital (200,000 + 50,000)	250,000
Share premium (40,000 + 30,000)	70,000
General reserve (20,000 + 5,000)	25,000

94

Mark up = 51.67%

	£
Sales (£130,000 × 140%)	182,000
Cost of sales (2 × £60,000)	120,000
Gross profit	62,000

$$\text{Mark up} = \frac{62,000}{120,000} = 51.67\%$$

95

Mark up = 60%

	£
Sales (160% of cost of sales)	240,000
Cost of sales (£240,000/1.6)	150,000
Gross profit	90,000

$$\text{Mark up} = \frac{90,000}{150,000} = 60\%$$

96

$$\text{Gearing} = \frac{\text{Prior charge capital}}{\text{Total capital}} \times 100\%$$

$$= \frac{10}{48}$$

$$= 20.8\%$$

97

$$\text{ROCE} = \frac{\text{Profit before interest and tax}}{\text{Average capital employed}} \times 100\%$$

$$= \frac{5.6(\text{W1})}{46.25(\text{W2})} \times 100\%$$

$$= 12.1\%$$

Workings

1   *Profit before interest and tax*

	£m
Profit before interest and tax (bal. fig.)	5.6
Interest (10 × 6%)	0.6
Tax	1.0
Profit after tax	4.0

2   *Average capital employed*

	£m
Capital at end of year	48.0
Retained profit (4 – 0.5)	3.5
Capital at start of year	44.5

$$\therefore \text{Average capital employed} = \frac{48 + 44.5}{2} = £46.25\text{m}$$

98

The gross profit margin is

	20X4	20X5
2,600/14,400	18.1%	
4,400/17,000		25.9%

99

The net profit margin is

	20X4	20X5
1,400/14,400	9.7%	
2,400/17,000		14.1%

100

The return on capital employed is

	20X4	20X5
(2,600 - 1,000)/6,700	23.9%	
2,400/5,720		42.0%

101

The acid test ratio is

	20X4	20X5
(2,000 + 2,400)/1,500	2.9:1	
(1,600 + 820)/2,700		0.9:1

102

The asset turnover is

	20X4	20X5
14,400/6,700	2.1 times	
17,000/5,720		3.0 times

103

The stock turnover period in days is

	20X4	20X5
1,300/11,800 × 365	40 days	
2,000/12,600 × 365		58 days

104

The gearing ratio is

	20X4	20X5
2,600/6,700 × 100	38.9 %	0 %

Pre-assessment tests

PRE ASSESSMENT TEST 1

---

1 Which of the following does **not** describe the historical cost convention:

A   Machinery is valued at depreciated original cost
B   Stock is valued on the FIFO or weighted average cost method
C   Properties are revalued to market value
D   Stock is valued at the lower of cost and net realisable value

---

2 FRS 18 specifies *four* qualities that financial statements should have. These are: Relevance, Reliability, Comparability and …

A   Accuracy
B   Consistency
C   Understandability
D   Materiality

---

3 The balance on a business's cash book at 31 March was a credit balance of £458.23. At that date there were unpresented cheques of £238.48 and outstanding lodgements of £331.66. What was the balance on the bank statement at 31 March?

A   £365.05 in credit
B   £365.05 overdrawn
C   £551.41 in credit
D   £551.41 overdrawn

---

4 During the quarter ending 30 June a business made sales of £288,909 inclusive of VAT and purchases of £165,000 exclusive of VAT. How much VAT is due to Customs and Excise at 30 June?

A   £14,154
B   £21,684
C   £28,875
D   £43,029

---

5 If an accountant encountered a situation where application of the materiality concept appeared to conflict with prudence, what course of action should he follow?

A   Materiality takes precedence
B   Prudence prevails
C   Ignore both of them
D   Make the financial information as 'neutral' as possible

---

6 At the start of May there was an accrual for telephone charges of £126.50 and the line rental had been prepaid by £30.00. At the end of May there were accruals for call charges of £152.78 and prepayment of line rental of £60.00. A bill for £462.52 was paid during the month. What is the telephone charge for the month of May in the profit and loss account?

A   £273.24
B   £458.80
C   £466.24
D   £651.80

---

7 A business depreciates its machinery at 20% on cost on the straight line basis and its motor vehicles at 30% on the reducing balance basis. The relevant balances in the trial balance at 30 June are as follows:

	£
Machinery at cost	125,300
Motor vehicles at cost	73,450
Machinery – accumulated depreciation	62,400
Motor vehicles – accumulated depreciation	34,750

Depreciation for the year has not yet been charged.

What is the net book value of fixed assets that will appear in the balance sheet?

A   £36,670
B   £54,505
C   £64,930
D   £162,080

---

8   The following information is known about the three lines of stock that a business has at the end of its accounting year:

	Cost per unit	Selling price per unit	Selling costs per unit	Units in stock
	£	£	£	
A	35.70	48.60	4.40	100
B	21.50	27.40	6.20	200
C	18.70	23.60	4.40	150

What is the value of stock in the balance sheet at the year end?

A   £10,615
B   £10,675
C   £11,540
D   £13,880

The following information relates to questions 9 and 10.

A business has the following summarised accounts.

Profit and loss account for the year ended 30 September 20X2

	£
Sales	100,400
Cost of sales	63,200
Gross profit	37,200
Expenses	16,700
Profit before tax	20,500
Tax	4,100
Profit after tax	16,400

Included in cost of sales is depreciation of £15,900.

Balance sheet as at	30 September 20X2	30 September 20X1
Fixed assets	93,200	77,600
Current assets:		
Stock	10,400	8,300
Debtors	16,800	17,900
Bank	2,100	4,500
	29,300	30,700
Creditors: amounts falling due within one year	17,900	20,100
Net current assets	11,400	10,600
	104,600	88,200
Share capital	50,000	50,000
Share premium	10,000	10,000
Profit and loss account	44,600	28,200
	104,600	88,200

During the year fixed assets with a cost of £4,800 were sold for £3,000 at a profit of £200.

9   What is the cash flow from operating activities?

    A   £33,000
    B   £33,200
    C   £39,400
    D   £39,800

10   What was the cash outflow on expenditure on fixed assets?

    A   £15,600
    B   £18,400
    C   £34,300
    D   £37,100

PRE ASSESSMENT TEST 2

1   Which of the following would **not** be categorised as capital expenditure?

    A   Purchase of a new building at a cost of £100,000
    B   Legal fees of £5,000 relating to the purchase of the building
    C   Installation of new air-conditioning system in the building
    D   Re-decoration of the building

2   The 'bedrocks' of accounting per FRS 18 are:

    A   Prudence and accruals
    B   Accruals and going concern
    C   Going concern and prudence
    D   Accruals and consistency

3   A business has paid wages by cheque of £74,500 during the month. Deductions of £13,800 for PAYE and £10,400 for employee's National Insurance were made. The employer's National Insurance for the period was £11,200. What is the wages cost figure to appear in the profit and loss account for the month?

    A   £74,500
    B   £98,700
    C   £99,500
    D   £109,900

4   Which of these would not be considered a change of accounting policy?

    A   A change from straight line to reducing balance method of depreciation
    B   A change of stock valuation method from AVCO to FIFO
    C   A revaluation of freehold properties
    D   Depreciation had been shown as part of cost of sales, now it is being presented under administrative expenses

5   A business had debtors at 31 March 20X1 of £78,300. During the year to 31 March 20X2 credit sales totalled £485,600 and £490,300 was received from credit customers. A bad debt of £5,600 was written off during the year and the provision for doubtful debts is to remain at 2% of the debtors figure.

    What is the charge for bad and doubtful debts to the profit and loss account for the year ended 31 March 20X2?

    A   £5,394
    B   £5,600
    C   £5,806
    D   £6,960

6   A business had a balance on its suspense account which was caused by the two following errors in the double entry.

    •   discounts allowed of £480 had been entered into the wrong side of the discounts allowed account
    •   telephone expenses of £468 had been entered into the telephone account as £648

    Once these two errors had been corrected there was no remaining balance on the suspense account.

    What was the original balance on the suspense account?

    A   £780 debit
    B   £780 credit
    C   £1,140 debit
    D   £1,140 credit

7   Given below is an extract from the trial balance of a manufacturing company:

	£
Direct factory labour	355,400
Indirect factory labour	58,200
Factory supervisor's salary	16,800
Opening stock of raw materials	21,500
Heat, light and power	30,500
Purchases of raw materials	169,300
Depreciation charge for factory machinery	18,200
Factory cleaning costs	21,400
Closing stock of raw materials	19,800

What is the prime cost of production?

The following information relates to questions 8 to 10.

Given below is a profit and loss account for a business for the year ended 30 June and a balance sheet at that date.

Profit and loss account

	£
Sales	258,300
Cost of sales	160,140
Gross profit	98,160
Operating expenses	51,660
Interest	6,600
Profit before tax	39,900
Tax	9,800
Profit after tax	30,100
Dividends	5,000
Retained profit	25,100

Balance sheet

	£	£
Fixed assets		551,000
Current assets		
Stock	24,000	
Debtors	53,800	
Cash	4,200	
	82,000	
Creditors: amounts falling due within one year		
Trade creditors	28,400	
Tax	5,000	
	33,400	
Net current assets		48,600
		599,600
Creditors: amounts falling due after more than one year		
Long term loan		100,000
		499,600
Share capital		300,000
Share premium		80,000
Profit and loss account		119,600
		499,600

Pre-assessment tests

In the table below enter the relevant monetary amounts to calculate the following ratios:

8	Net profit percentage	=		/		× 100
		=				
9	Return on capital employed	=		/		× 100
		=				
10	Stock turnover days	=		/		× 365
		=				

Answers to pre-assessment tests

PRE-ASSESSMENT TEST 1

1   C   All of the others are concerned with valuation at cost.

2   C   Understandability

3   D

	£	
Cash book balance	458.23	overdrawn
Less: unpresented cheques	(238.48)	
Add: outstanding lodgements	331.66	
	551.41	overdrawn

4   A

	£
Output VAT (288,909 × 17.5/117.5)	43,029
Input VAT (165,000 × 17.5%)	(28,875)
VAT due	14,154

5   D   FRS 18 requires that financial information should be neutral, ie free from bias, and present a true and fair view.

6   B

Telephone expenses account

	£		£
Opening prepayment	30.00	Opening accrual	126.50
Cash paid	462.52	Profit and loss account	458.80
Closing accrual	152.78	Closing prepayment	60.00
	645.30		645.30

7   C

	£
Machinery - cost	125,300
Accumulated depreciation (62,400 + (125,300 × 20%))	87,460
NBV	37,840
Motor vehicles - cost	73,450
Accumulated depreciation (34,750 + (73,450 - 34,750) × 30%))	46,360
NBV	27,090
Total NBV (37,840 + 27,090)	64,930

8   A

	Cost	NRV	Quantity	Value
A	35.70	44.20	100	3,570
D	21.50	21.20	200	4,240
C	18.70	19.20	150	2,805
				10,615

9   A

	£
Operating profit	20,500
Add: depreciation	15,900
Less: profit on sale	(200)
Increase in stocks	(2,100)
Decrease in debtors	1,100
Decrease in creditors	(2,200)
Net cash flow from operating activities	33,000

10   C

Fixed assets at NBV

	£		£
Opening balance	77,600	Disposal (3,000 – 200)	2,800
		Depreciation	15,900
Additions (bal fig)	34,300	Closing balance	93,200
	111,900		111,900

PRE-ASSESSMENT TEST 2

1   D

All of the other three options are either part of the cost of buying the building or necessary to get it into operational condition.

2   B   Accruals and going concern are the 'bedrocks'.

The other concepts are 'desirable features'.

3   D

	£
Net wages	74,500
PAYE	13,800
Employee's NIC	10,400
Employer's NIC	11,200
	109,900

4   A   This is a change of estimation technique.

The others are all changes of measurement basis or presentation.

5   A

Debtors control account

	£		£
		Bad debt written off	5,600
Opening balance	78,300	Cash received	490,300
Credit sales	485,600	Closing balance	68,000
	563,900		563,900

	£
Opening provision for doubtful debts (78,300 × 2%)	1,566
Closing provision for doubtful debts (68,000 × 2%)	1,360
Decrease in provision	206

Bad debts expense

	£		£
Bad debt written off	5,600	Decrease in provision	206
		Profit and loss account	5,394
	5,600		5,600

6   A   Double entry to correct errors:

		£	£
Debit	Discounts allowed (£480 × 2)	960	
Credit	Suspense		960

		£	£
Debit	Suspense (648 – 468)	180	
Credit	Telephone		180

Suspense account

	£		£
Telephone	180	Discounts	960
Opening balance (bal fig)	780		
	960		960

7   The prime cost of production is £526,400.

		£
Opening stock of raw materials		21,500
Purchases of raw materials		169,300
		190,800
Less: closing stock of raw materials		(19,800)
Direct materials used		171,000
Direct factory labour		355,400
Prime cost of production		526,400

8   Net profit percentage   =   46,500/258,300   × 100

                                   =   18.0%

9   Return on capital employed   =   46,500/599,600   × 100

                                   =   7.8%

10   Stock turnover days   =   24,000/160,140   × 365

                                   =   54.7 days

Mock Assessments

Paper 1

Financial Accounting Fundamentals

FAFN

INSTRUCTIONS TO CANDIDATES

You are allowed one and a half hours to answer this question paper.
Answer all 40 questions on this paper.

**DO NOT OPEN THIS PAPER UNTIL YOU ARE READY
TO START UNDER EXAMINATION CONDITIONS**

ANSWER *ALL* 40 QUESTIONS

1   An imprest system is

A   Accounting computer software
B   An audit process
C   Automatic agreement of the cash book and bank statement
D   A method of controlling petty cash

2   Which ONE of the following is correct?

A   All limited companies are required by law to have an external audit
B   Only public limited companies are required by law to have an external audit
C   Only limited companies above a certain size are required by law to have an external audit
D   An external audit for a limited company is voluntary

3   At 31 March 20X1, accrued rent payable was £300. During the year ended 31 March 20X2, rent paid was £4,000, including an invoice for £1,200 for the quarter ended 30 April 20X2. What is the profit and loss account charge for rent payable for the year ended 31 March 20X2?

A   £3,300   B   £3,900   C   £4,100   D   £4,700

4   The responsibility for internal control rests with

A   The internal auditors
B   The external auditors
C   The shareholders
D   The directors

5   The annual insurance premium for S Ltd for the period 1 July 20X1 to 30 June 20X2 is £13,200, which is 10% more than the previous year. Insurance premiums are paid on 1 July.

What is the profit and loss account charge for the year ended 31 December 20X1?

A   £11,800   B   £12,540   C   £12,600   D   £13,200

6   A bank reconciliation showed the following differences between the bank statement and the cash book.

Unpresented cheques of   £750
Outstanding deposits of   £500
Bank charges of   £100

If the balance on the bank statement is £1,000 overdrawn, what is the balance in the cash book before any adjustments?

A   Debit £250   B   Credit £1,150   C   Credit £1,250   D   Credit £1,500

7   Which ONE of the following expenses should be included in prime cost in a manufacturing account?

A   Repairs to factory machinery
B   Direct production wages
C   Office salaries
D   Factory insurance

8   The entries in a sales ledger control account are:

	£
Sales	250,000
Bank	225,000
Returns	2,500
Bad debts	3,000
Returned unpaid cheque	3,500
Contra purchase ledger account	4,000

What is the balance on the sales ledger control account?

A   £12,000   B   £19,000   C   £25,000   D   £27,000

9   A Ltd has an item in stock which cost £1,000 and can be sold for £1,200. However, before it can be sold, it will require to be modified at a cost of £150. The expected selling costs of the item are an additional £100.

How should this item be valued in stock?

A   £950   B   £1,000   C   £1,050   D   £1,100

10   A 'value for money' audit is:

A   An external audit with limited scope.
B   A review of expenditure to ensure effectiveness, efficiency and economy.
C   A voluntary audit by an unregistered auditor.
D   None of these.

11   Which ONE of the following statements regarding a fixed assets register is NOT correct?

A   A fixed assets register enables reconciliation to be made with the nominal ledger
B   A fixed assets register enables depreciation charges to be posted to the nominal ledger
C   A fixed assets register agrees with the fixed asset nominal ledger account
D   A fixed assets register records the physical location of an asset

12   B Ltd purchased a machine for £120,000 on 1 October 20X1. The estimated useful life is 4 years with a residual value of £4,000. B Ltd uses the straight-line method for depreciation and charges depreciation on a monthly basis.

What is the charge for depreciation for the year ended 31 December 20X1?

A   £7,250   B   £7,500   C   £29,000   D   £30,000

13   In the quarter ended 31 March 20X2, C Ltd had VAT taxable outputs, net of VAT, of £90,000 and taxable inputs, net of VAT, of £72,000.

If the rate of VAT is 10%, how much VAT is due?

A   £1,800 receivable   B   £2,000 receivable   C   £1,800 payable   D   £2,000 payable

14   Which of the following statements concerning a 'true and fair view' is correct?

A   True and fair has a precise definition which is universally accepted
B   There can only be one true and fair view of a company's financial statements
C   True and fair means the financial statements are correct
D   True and fair is mainly determined by compliance with generally accepted accounting practice

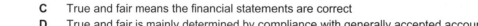

15   The M Club discloses the following note to its Income and Expenditure Account:

'Subscriptions in arrears are accounted for when received; subscriptions in advance are accounted for on a matching basis.'

At 31 March 20X1, there were subscriptions owing of £1,000 and subscriptions in advance of £500. During the year ended 31 March 20X2, subscriptions of £10,000 were received, including subscriptions relating to the previous year of £800 and subscriptions in advance of £600.

What amount should be included for subscriptions in the year ended 31 March 20X2?

A	£8,100	**B**	£8,900	**C**	£9,100	**D**	£9,900

16   The total cost of salaries charged to the profit and loss account is:

A   The total gross salaries plus employer's national insurance contributions
B   The total gross salaries
C   The total net salaries
D   The total net salaries plus employer's national insurance contributions

17   The segregation of duties is

A   Delegation of duties by a manager
B   Two staff sharing one job
C   A feature of internal control
D   All of the above

18   The net profit percentage in a company is 12% and the asset turnover ratio is 2.

What is the return on capital employed?

A	6%	**B**	10%	**C**	14%	**D**	24%

19   Which of the following are used in a coding system for accounting transactions?

A   Department code
B   Nominal ledger code
C   Product code
D   All of the above

20   APM Ltd provides the following note to fixed assets in its balance sheet.

Plant and machinery

	Cost	Depreciation	Net book value
	£'000	£'000	£'000
Opening balance	25	12	13
Additions/charge	15	4	11
Disposals	(10)	(8)	(2)
Closing balance	30	8	22

The additional machinery was purchased for cash. A machine was sold at a profit of £2,000.

What is the net cash outflow for plant and machinery?

A	£9,000	**B**	£11,000	**C**	£13,000	**D**	£15,000

21   Which of the following errors will cause the trial balance totals to be unequal?

    A   Errors of transposition
    B   Errors of omission
    C   Errors of principle
    D   All of the above

22   Which ONE of the following is a record of prime entry?

    A   The nominal ledger
    B   The sales ledger
    C   The trial balance
    D   The sales day book

23   P is a sole proprietor whose accounting records are incomplete. All the sales are cash sales and during the year £50,000 was banked, including £5,000 from the sale of a business car. He paid £12,000 wages in cash from the till and withdrew £2,000 per month as drawings. The cash in the till at the beginning and end of the year was £300 and £400 respectively.

What were the sales for the year?

    A   £80,900   **B**   £81,000   **C**   £81,100   **D**   £86,100

24   Which of the following is NOT helpful in detecting an error?

    A   A bank reconciliation
    B   A sales ledger control account
    C   An imprest system
    D   A suspense account

25   Which ONE of the following is an appropriation by a limited company?

    A   Directors' salaries
    B   Dividends
    C   Donation to a charity
    D   Loan interest

26   At the year end of SED Ltd in December 20X0, a journal entry was raised to accrue for utility expenses of £3,600. This journal entry was reversed in January 20X1. During the year ended December 20X1, £30,000 was paid for utility expenses, of which £4,000 was prepaid at the year end.

The charge to the profit and loss account for utility expenses for the year ended December 20X1 was

£

27   Z Ltd's cash book shows a credit balance of £2,200. A comparison with the bank statement showed the following:

    (i)   unpresented cheques totalling £600;

    (ii)   receipts of £1,200 not yet cleared by the bank;

    (iii)   bank charges of £300 not entered in the cash book;

    (iv)   a cheque from a customer for £400, which had been entered in the cash book when received, has now been returned by the bank as 'dishonoured'.

The overdraft balance on Z Ltd's bank statement is £

The following data relates to questions 28 and 29.

On the first day of Month 1, a business had prepaid insurance of £10,000. On the first day of Month 8, it paid in full the annual insurance invoice of £36,000, to cover the following year.

28   The amount charged in the profit and loss account for insurance for the year is £ ▇▇▇▇▇▇▇

29   The amount shown in the balance sheet at the year end is £ ▇▇▇▇▇▇▇

30   SSG Ltd bought a machine for £40,000 in January 19W8. The machine had an expected useful life of six years and an expected residual value of £10,000. The machine was depreciated on the straight-line basis. In December 20X1, the machine was sold for £15,000. The company has a policy in its internal accounts of combining the depreciation charge with the profit or loss on disposal of assets.

The total amount of depreciation and profit/loss charged to the internal profit and loss account over the life of the machine was £ ▇▇▇▇▇▇

31   DEF plc has a supplier, M Ltd, and the balance on M Ltd's purchase ledger account at 31 July 20X2 was a credit balance of £2,000. On 5 August 20X2, DEF plc received the July statement from M Ltd showing a balance due of £3,000. The purchase ledger supervisor investigates the difference and discovers that:

(i)   an invoice for £2,000 from M Ltd dated 31 July was not entered in the purchase ledger account until 3 August 20X2, but appears on M Ltd's July statement.

(ii)   a cheque for £600 sent from DEF plc to M Ltd on 25 July 20X2 in payment of a July invoice does not appear on M Ltd's July statement. This cheque was presented by M Ltd on 31 July 20X2.

The purchase ledger supervisor at DEF plc contacts the sales ledger supervisor at M Ltd and correctly says that there is a difference between the ledger accounts of £ ▇▇▇▇▇▇

32   On 1 October 20X2, the debtors' balance at G Ltd was £80,000. A summary of the transactions in the month of October is set out below.

	£
Cheques received	100,000
Contra creditors	6,000
Sales	90,000
Returns inwards	4,000
Discounts allowed	10,000

The debtors' balance at 31 October was £ ▇▇▇▇▇▇

33   SAD plc paid £240,000 in net wages to its employees in August 20X2. Employees' tax was £24,000, employees' national insurance was £12,000 and employer's national insurance was £14,000. Employees had contributed £6,000 to a pension scheme and had voluntarily asked for £3,000 to be deducted for charitable giving.

The amount to be charged to the profit and loss account in August 20X2 for wages is £ ▇▇▇▇▇▇

34   At the beginning of Period 6, XYZ Ltd had opening stock of 20 units of product X valued at £4.00 each. During Period 6, the following stock movements occurred:

Day 5   Sold 15 items for £5.00 each
Day 10   Bought 8 items for £6.00 each
Day 14   Sold 12 items for £7.00 each

Using the FIFO method of stock valuation, the closing stock at the end of Period 6 was £ [   ]

The following data relates to questions 35 to 37.

The accounts for SPA plc are set out below.

Profit and loss account for the year ended 30 November 20X2

	£'000	£'000
Turnover		5,000
Opening stock	200	
Purchases	3,100	
Closing stock	(300)	
Cost of sales		(3,000)
Gross profit		2,000
Operating expenses		(500)
Operating profit		1,500

Balance sheet at 30 November 20X2

	£'000	£'000
Fixed assets		3,000
Current assets		
Stock	300	
Debtors	900	
Bank	50	
	1,250	
Current liabilities		
Trade creditors	(250)	
		1,000
		4,000
Share capital		2,000
Profit and loss account		2,000
		4,000

35   The return on capital employed in SPA plc is [   ]

36   The fixed asset turnover ratio in SPA plc is [   ]

37   The quick ratio (acid test ratio) in SPA plc is [   ]

38   Tanwir commenced his business on 1 October 20X9, with capital in the bank of £20,000. During his first month of trading, his transactions were as follows.

1 October	Purchase stocks for £3,500 on credit from A Jones
3 October	Paid £1,200 rental of premises, by cheque
5 October	Paid £5,000 for office equipment, by cheque
10 October	Sold goods costing £1,000 for £1,750, on credit to P Duncan
15 October	Returned stocks costing £500 to A Jones
18 October	Purchased stocks for £2,400 on credit from A Jones
25 October	Paid A Jones for the net purchases of 1 October, by cheque
28 October	P Duncan paid £500 on account, by cheque

The balance on the account of A Jones at 31 October 20X9 was £ ▢.

The following data relates to questions 39 and 40.

During his first year of trading, Tanwir brings his private car, valued at £6,000 into the business as well as his initial £20,000 of capital. The business made a net profit of £17,500 for the year, after deducting £650 for petrol which was paid out of his private funds. He has drawn £5,000 out of the business bank account for himself, as well as paying his home telephone bill of £450 from business funds.

39   Tanwir's capital at the end of his first year of trading was £ ▢.

40   State the accounting concept which has governed the treatment of the items which make up Tanwir's capital at the end of the year. ▢

MOCK ASSESSMENT 1
ANSWERS

DO NOT TURN THIS PAGE UNTIL YOU
HAVE COMPLETED THE MOCK ASSESSMENT

1   D   A method of controlling petty cash.

2   C   Only limited companies above a certain size are required to have an external audit.

3   A

RENT PAYABLE

	£		£
Rent paid	4,000	Balance b/d - accrual	300
		Profit and loss charge	3,300
		Balance c/d - prepayment	
		(1,200 × 1/3)	400
	4,000		4,000

4   D   This is part of their stewardship function.

5   C

	£
1 Jan - 30 June (12,000 × 6/12)	6,000
1 July - 31 Dec (13,200 × 6/12)	6,600
	12,600

6   B

	£
Bank statement balance	1,000 o/d
Less: bank charges	(100)
Add: unpresented cheques	750
Less: outstanding deposits	(500)
Balance per cash book	1,150 o/d

7   B   Only **direct** production costs are included in prime cost.

8   B

SALES LEDGER CONTROL ACCOUNT

	£		£
Sales	250,000	Bank	225,000
Unpaid cheque	3,500	Returns	2,500
		Bad debts	3,000
		Contra	4,000
		Balance c/d	19,000
	253,500		253,500

9   A

	£
Cost	1,000
Selling price	1,200
Less: modification costs	(150)
Less: selling costs	(100)
Net realisable value	950

10   B   This is normally carried out by internal auditors.

11   C   The fixed asset register should agree with the nominal ledger but will not necessarily always agree if there are either errors in the register or in the nominal ledger.

12   A

$$\text{Annual depreciation} \quad = \frac{\pounds120,000 - 4,000}{4 \text{ years}}$$

$$= \pounds29,000$$

Depreciation charge 1 Oct - 31 Dec $= \pounds29,000 \times 3/12$

$$= \pounds7,250$$

13   C

	£
Output VAT (£90,000 × 10%)	9,000
Input VAT (£72,000 × 10%)	(7,200)
	1,800 payable

14   D   True and fair is mainly determined by compliance with GAAP

15   D

SUBSCRIPTIONS ACCOUNT

	£		£
Income and expenditure a/c	9,900	Balance b/d - subs in advance	500
Balance c/d - subs in advance	600	Bank	10,000
	10,500		10,500

16   A   Employer's NI contributions are not deducted from gross salaries – they are an additional cost.

17   C   An internal control procedure designed to prevent certain types of fraud.

18   D

Return on capital employed   = Net profit % × asset turnover

$$= 12\% \times 2$$

$$= 24\%$$

19   D   It is entirely possible that a coding system would identify the department and product to which the transaction relates as well as the nominal ledger code for posting. The department and product codes would be of most use for management accounting purposes.

20   B

FIXED ASSETS AT COST

	£'000		£'000
Balance b/d	25	Disposal	10
Additions (bal fig)	15	Balance c/d	30
	40		40

	£'000
Disposal - net book value	2
Profit on disposal	2
Proceeds	4

Net cash inflow   = £15,000 – 4,000

$$= \pounds11,000$$

21 **A**   B and C will not give rise to any numerical imbalance.

22 **D**   The sales day book.

23 **C**

CASH ACCOUNT

	£		£
Balance b/d	300	Bankings (50,000 - 5,000)	45,000
		Wages	12,000
		Drawings	24,000
Takings (bal fig)	81,100	Balance c/d	400
	81,400		81,400

24 **D**   A suspense account is a location where some accumulated errors may be recorded, but it is not a method of detecting errors.

25 **B**   Dividends are an appropriation. All of the others are expenses of the business.

26   £22,400

(£30,000 – £3,600 – £4,000)

27   £3,500

	£
Cash book balance	(2,200)
Bank charges	(300)
Dishonoured cheque	(400)
Amended cash book balance	(2,900)
Unpresented cheques	600
Outstanding lodgements	(1,200)
Bank statement balance	(3,500)

28   £25,000

£10,000 + (£36,000 × 5/12) = £25,000

29   £21,000

£36,000 × 7/12 = £21,000

30   £25,000

$$\text{Annual depreciation} = \frac{£40,000 - £10,000}{6}$$

$$= £5,000$$

4 years depreciation = £20,000

	£
Net book value in Dec 2001 = £40,000 – £20,000	20,000
Disposal proceeds	15,000
Loss on disposal	5,000

Total depreciation and loss on disposal = £20,000 + £5,000

= £25,000

31   £1,600

	£
DEF balance	2,000
Additional invoice	2,000
Amended balance	4,000
M Ltd balance	3,000
Less: cheque payment	(600)
	2,400

Difference remaining = £4,000 - £2,400

= £1,600

32   £50,000

Debtors account

	£		£
Opening balance	80,000	Contra	6,000
Sales	90,000	Cheques received	100,000
		Returns inwards	4,000
		Discounts allowed	10,000
		Closing balance	50,000
	170,000		170,000

33   £299,000

	£
Net wages	240,000
Employee's tax	24,000
Employee's NI	12,000
Pension scheme contributions	6,000
Charitable donations	3,000
Gross wages	285,000
Employer's NI	14,000
	299,000

34   £6.00

Opening stock	20 units @ £4.00
Day 5 sale	15 units costing £4.00
Remaining	5 units @ £4.00
Day 10 purchase	8 units @ £6.00
Day 14 sale	5 units @ £4.00
	7 units @ £6.00
Remaining	1 unit @ £6.00

35   37.5%

$$\text{Return on capital employed} = \frac{\text{Operating profit}}{\text{Share captial} + \text{reserves}} \times 100$$

$$= \frac{1,500}{4,000} \times 100$$

$$= 37.5\%$$

36   1.67 : 1

$$\text{Fixed asset turnover ratio} = \frac{\text{Turnover}}{\text{Fixed assets}}$$

$$= \frac{5,000}{3,000}$$

$$= 1.67 : 1$$

37   3.8 : 1

$$\text{Quick ratio} = \frac{\text{Current assets} - \text{stock}}{\text{Current liabilities}}$$

$$= \frac{1,250 - 300}{250}$$

$$= 3.8 : 1$$

38   Balance = £2,400

A JONES

		£				£
15.10	Returns	500	1.10	Purchases		3,500
25.10	Bank	3,000	18.10	Purchases		2,400
31.10	Balance c/d	2,400				
		5,900				5,900

39   Tanwir's capital = £38,700

	£
Cash introduced on 1 October 20X9	20,000
Car introduced	6,000
Profit for the year	17,500
Petrol paid for privately	650
Drawings	(5,000)
Home phone bill	(450)
Capital at the year end	38,700

40   The accounting concept which governs the treatment of capital is the entity concept. The entity concept ensures that the business is treated as a separate entity. Therefore every transaction made by Tanwir which affects the business must be recorded.

Paper 1

Financial Accounting Fundamentals

FAFN

INSTRUCTIONS TO CANDIDATES

You are allowed one and a half hours to answer this question paper.
Answer all 40 questions on this paper.

**DO NOT OPEN THIS PAPER UNTIL YOU ARE READY
TO START UNDER EXAMINATION CONDITIONS**

ANSWER **ALL** 40 QUESTIONS

---

1   Which ONE of the following best describes the stewardship function?

A   Ensuring high profits
B   Managing cash
C   Ensuring the recording, controlling and safeguarding of assets
D   Ensuring high dividends to shareholders

---

2   External auditors are primarily responsible for

A   writing a report to the shareholders expressing an opinion on the financial statements
B   preparing the financial statements
C   detecting errors and fraud
D   ensuring that the accounts show a true and fair view

---

3   When preparing financial statements in periods of inflation, directors

A   Must reduce asset values
B   Must increase asset values
C   Must reduce dividends
D   Need make no adjustments

---

4   The following information relates to a bank reconciliation.

(i)   The bank balance in the cashbook before taking the items below into account was £8,970 overdrawn.

(ii)   Bank charges of £550 on the bank statement have not been entered in the cashbook.

(iii)   The bank has credited the account in error with £425 which belongs to another customer.

(iv)   Cheque payments totalling £3,275 have been entered in the cashbook but have not been presented for payment.

(v)   Cheques totalling £5,380 have been correctly entered on the debit side of the cashbook but have not been paid in at the bank.

What was the balance as shown by the bank statement *before* taking the items above into account?

A   £8,970 overdrawn
B   £11,200 overdrawn
C   £12,050 overdrawn
D   £17,750 overdrawn

---

5   W Ltd bought a new printing machine from abroad. The cost of the machine was £80,000. The installation costs were £5,000 and the employees received specific training on how to use this particular machine, at a cost of £2,000. Before using the machine to print customers' orders, a test was undertaken and the paper and ink cost £1,000.

What should be the cost of the machine in the company's balance sheet?

A   £80,000
B   £85,000
C   £87,000
D   £88,000

6   In a manual accounting system, the most important reason for extracting a trial balance prior to preparing financial statements is that

   A   it proves the arithmetical accuracy of the ledgers.
   B   it provides a summary of the financial statements.
   C   it proves the individual ledger accounts are correct.
   D   it reveals how errors have been made.

7   JSL Ltd operates the imprest system for its petty cash with a float of $750. At the end of July, the cashier prepared a spreadsheet for the petty cash expenses with a total column and analysis columns. A cash voucher for petrol for $50 was incorrectly entered as $5 in the total column and also in one of the analysis columns in the spreadsheet. The total column was posted to the cash account, the analysis columns were posted to the relevant nominal ledger accounts and cash was drawn from the bank for the total of the cash expenditure on the spreadsheet.

   The effect of this error would be

   A   a petty cash balance of $705.
   B   petrol expenses overstated by $45.
   C   an imbalance on the trial balance.
   D   a petty cash balance of $750.

8   The electricity account for the year ended 30 June 20X1 was as follows.

	£
Opening balance for electricity accrued at 1 July 20X0	300
Payments made during the year	
1 August 20X0 for three months to 31 July 20X0	600
1 November 20X0 for three months to 31 October 20X0	720
1 February 20X1 for three months to 31 January 20X1	900
30 June 20X1 for three months to 30 April 20X1	840

   Which of the following is the appropriate entry for electricity?

	Accrued	Charge to profit and loss account
	At 30 June 20X1	year ended 30 June 20X1
A	£Nil	£3,060
B	£460	£3,320
C	£560	£3,320
D	£560	£3,420

9   The year end of M plc is 30 November 20X0. The company pays for its gas by a standing order of £600 per month. On 1 December 20W9, the statement from the gas supplier showed that M plc had overpaid by £200. M plc received gas bills for the four quarters commencing on 1 December 20W9 and ending on 30 November 20X0 for £1,300, £1,400, £2,100 and £2,000 respectively.

   Which of the following is the correct charge for gas in M plc's profit and loss account for the year ended 30 November 20X0?

   A   £6,800
   B   £7,000
   C   £7,200
   D   £7,400

10 S & Co. sell three products – Basic, Super and Luxury. The following information was available at the year end.

	Basic	Super	Luxury
	£ per unit	£ per unit	£ per unit
Original cost	6	9	18
Estimated selling price	9	12	15
Selling and distribution costs	1	4	5
	units	units	units
Units of stock	200	250	150

The value of stock at the year end should be

A   £4,200
B   £4,700
C   £5,700
D   £6,150

11 A car was purchased by a newsagent business in May 20X7 for:

	£
Cost	10,000
Road tax	150
Total	10,150

The business adopts a date of 31 December as its year end.

The car was traded in for a replacement vehicle in August 20Y0 at an agreed value of £5,000.

It has been depreciated at 25% per annum on the reducing-balance method, charging a full year's depreciation in the year of purchase and none in the year of sale.

What was the profit or loss on disposal of the vehicle during the year ended December 20Y0?

A   Profit: £718
B   Profit: £781
C   Profit: £1,788
D   Profit: £1,836

12 A summary of the balance sheet of M Ltd at 31 March 20X0 was as follows

	£'000
Total assets less current liabilities	120
Ordinary share capital	40
Share premium account	10
Profit and loss account	10
5% debentures 20Y0	60
	120

If the operating profit for the year ended 31 March 20X0 was £15,000, what is the return on capital employed?

A   12.5%
B   25%
C   30%
D   37.5%

13 The annual sales of a company are £235,000 including VAT at 17.5%. Half of the sales are on credit terms; half are cash sales. The debtors in the balance sheet are £23,500.

What are the debtor days (to the nearest day)?

A   37 days
B   43 days
C   73 days
D   86 days

14   The concept of capital maintenance is important for

    A   The sources of finance
    B   The measurement of profit
    C   The relationship of debt to equity
    D   The purchase of fixed assets

15   Internal control includes 'detect' controls and 'prevent' controls. Which of the following is a detect control?

    A   Signing overtime claim forms
    B   Matching purchase invoices with goods received notes
    C   Preparing bank reconciliations
    D   Matching sales invoices with delivery notes

16   A stock record card shows the following details.

February	1	50 units in stock at a cost of £40 per unit
	7	100 units purchased at a cost of £45 per unit
	14	80 units sold
	21	50 units purchased at a cost of £50 per unit
	28	60 units sold

What is the value of stock at 28 February using the FIFO method?

    A   £2,450
    B   £2,700
    C   £2,950
    D   £3,000

17   The year end for ABC Ltd is July 20X2 and in that month a company car was stolen. The net book value of the company car was $8,000, but the company expects the insurance company to pay only $6,000. The correct journal entry to record this information was entered in the books in July 20X2. In August 20X2 the insurance company sent a cheque for $6,500.

The journal entry to record this is:

		Dr $	*Cr* $
A	Bank	6,500	
	Sundry debtor		6,500
B	Bank	6,500	
	Sundry debtor		6,000
	Disposal of fixed assets account		500
C	Bank	500	
	Disposal of fixed assets account		500
D	Bank	500	
	Sundry debtor		500

18   The trial balance of EHL plc does not balance and the debits exceed the credits by $2,300. The following errors are discovered:

- the single column manual cash book receipts column was undercast by $600;
- discount received of $400 had been debited to the interest payable account;
- the proceeds of $1,000 on the sale of a fixed asset had been credited to sales.

Following the correction of these errors, the balance on the suspense account would be

    A Cr $900   **B** Cr $2,100   **C** Cr $3,700   **D** Dr $2,100

19 At the beginning of the year in GHI Ltd, the opening work-in-progress was $240,000. During the year, the following expenditure was incurred:

	$
Prime cost	720,000
Factory overheads	72,000
The closing work-in-progress was	350,000

The factory cost of goods completed during the year was

A	$538,000	B	$610,000	C	$682,000	D	$902,000

20 In July 20X2, a company sold goods at standard value added tax (VAT) rate with a net value of £200,000, goods exempt from VAT with a value of £50,000 and goods at zero VAT rate with a net value of £25,000. The purchases in July 20X2, which were all subject to VAT, were £161,000, including VAT. Assume that the rate of VAT is 15%.

The difference between VAT input tax and VAT output tax is

A	Dr £9,000	B	Cr £5,850	C	Cr £9,000	D	None of these

21 After the profit and loss account for Z Ltd had been prepared, it was found that accrued expenses of $1,500 had been omitted and that closing stock had been overvalued by $500.

The effect of these errors is an

A   overstatement of net profit of $1,000
B   overstatement of net profit of $2,000
C   understatement of net profit of $1,000
D   understatement of net profit of $2,000

22 The cashier is reconciling his company's cash book with the bank statement at 31 March 20X3.

	$
The firm's cash book shows a debit balance of	12,350

The following information is available:

	$
Bank charges not entered in the cash book	170
Unpresented cheques	4,600
Direct debit payment on the bank statement not entered in the cash book	230
Sales receipts banked, but not credited by the bank	9,400
A cheque from a customer which had previously been entered in the cash book when received, has been returned by the bank as 'dishonoured, and this has not been recorded in the cash book	110

What should be stated as the bank balance in the company's balance sheet at 31 March 20X3?

A	$11,840	B	$12,060	C	$12,860	D	$16,640

23 D is preparing the accounts for A Ltd for the year ended 31 March 20X3. The most recent gas bill received by A Ltd was dated 6 February 20X3 and related to the quarter 1 November 20X2 to 31 January 20X3, and the amount of the bill was $2,100.

Which ONE of the following ledger entries should be made in A Ltd's books at 31 March 20X3?

	Debit		*Credit*	
A	Accruals	Nil	Gas expense	Nil
B	Gas expense	$1,400	Accruals	$1,400
C	Accruals	$1,400	Gas expense	$1,400
D	Gas expense	$2,100	Accruals	$2,100

BPP
PROFESSIONAL EDUCATION

24   The following information related to Q plc for the year ended 28 February 20X3:

	$
Prime cost	122,000
Factory overheads	185,000
Opening work-in-progress at 1 March 20X2	40,000
Factory cost of goods completed	300,000

The closing work-in-progress at 28 February 20X3 was

   A $33,000   **B** $40,000   **C** $47,000   **D** $54,000

---

25   N Ltd, which is registered for VAT, received an invoice from an advertising agency for £4,000 plus VAT. The rat of VAT on the goods was 17.5%. The correct ledger entries are:

		Debit			Credit	
		£				£
A	Advertising expense	4,000		Creditors		4,000
B	Advertising expense	4,700		Creditors		4,700
C	Advertising expense	4,700		Creditors		4,000
				VAT account		700
D	Advertising expense	4,000		Creditors		4,700
	VAT account	700				

---

26   E Ltd received an invoice for the purchase of fixed asset equipment which was credited to the correct supplier's ledger account, but debited to the equipment repairs account, instead of the equipment account.

The effect of not correcting this error on the financial statements would be:

   A   Profit would be overstated and fixed assets would be understated.
   B   Profit would be overstated and fixed assets would be overstated.
   C   Profit would be understated and fixed assets would be overstated.
   D   Profit would be understated and fixed assets would be understated.

---

27   H Ltd began trading on 1 July 20X1. The company is now preparing its accounts for the accounting year ended 30 June 20X2. Rates are charged for a tax year, which runs from 1 April to 31 March, and were $1,800 for the year ended 31 March 20X2 and $2,000 for the year ended 31 March 20X3. Rates are payable quarterly in advance, plus any arrears, on 1 March, 1 June, 1 September and 1 December.

The charge to H Ltd's profit and loss account for rates for the year ended 30 June 20X2 is

   A $1,650   **B** $1,700   **C** $1,850   **D** $1,900

---

28   The return on capital employed for S plc is 24% and the net asset turnover ratio is 3 times.

What is the profit margin?

   A   8%   **B**   28%   **C**   72%   **D**   It cannot be calculated

---

29   The total cost of salaries charged to a limited company's profit and loss account is

   A   cash paid to employees
   B   net pay earned by employees
   C   gross pay earned by employees
   D   gross pay earned by employees, plus employer's national insurance contributions

30   The following is the aged debtors analysis for J Ltd at 30 April 20X3:

Age of debt	Less than 1 month	1-2 months	2-3 months	Over 3 months
Amount ($)	12,000	24,000	8,000	6,000

The company provides for doubtful debts as follows:

Provision	0%	1%	10%	30%

The doubtful debt provision at 1 May 20X2 brought forward was $2,880.

The entry for doubtful debts in the profit and loss account for the year ended 30 April 20X3 and the net debtors figure in the balance sheet at that date should be:

	Profit and loss account	Balance sheet
A	$40 credit	$47,160
B	$40 debit	$47,160
C	$2,840 debit	$50,000
D	$2,840 credit	$47,160

31   The prime cost of goods manufactured is the total of

A   raw materials consumed
B   raw materials consumed and direct wages
C   raw materials consumed, direct wages and direct expenses
D   raw materials consumed, direct wages, direct expenses and production overheads

32   On 1 May 20X3, E Ltd owed a supplier $1,200. During the month of May, E Ltd:

- purchased goods for $1,700 and the supplier offered a 5% discount for payment within the month
- returned goods value at $100 which had been purchased in April 20X3
- sent a cheque to the supplier for payment of the goods delivered in May

The balance on the supplier's account at the end of May 20X3 is:

A $1,015   B $1,100   C $1,185   D $1,300

33   The main advantage of using a sales ledger control account is that

A   double entry bookkeeping is not necessary
B   it helps in detecting errors
C   it helps with credit control
D   it ensures that the trial balance will always balance

34   The following information relates to J Ltd for the year ended 30 April 20X3.

	$'000
Retained profit for the year	28,000
Net cash inflow from operating activities	26,000
Dividend paid	3,000
Profit on sale of fixed assets	1,000
Proceeds on sale of fixed assets	5,000
Taxation paid	2,000
Interest paid	4,000
Payments for fixed assets	8,000
Issue of debentures	6,000

The cash flow statement will show

A   a decrease in cash of $13,000
B   an increase in cash of $14,000
C   an increase in cash of $20,000
D   an increase in cash of $22,000

35   Which of the following is an 'appropriation of profit' in a limited company?

    A   Interest paid
    B   Dividend paid
    C   Directors' remuneration
    D   Retained profit

36   N operates an imprest system for petty cash. On 1 February 20X3, the float was $300. It was decided that this should be increased to $375 at the end of February 20X3.

    During February, the cashier paid $20 for window cleaning, $100 for stationery and $145 for coffee and biscuits. The cashier received $20 from staff for the private use of the photocopier and $60 for a miscellaneous cash sale.

    What amount was drawn from the bank account for petty cash at the end of February 20X3?

    A $185   B $260   C $315   D $375

37   The following are extracts from the financial statements for the year ended 31 January 20X3 of M plc:

	$'000
Issued ordinary shares of $1	200
Share premium account	50
Profit and loss account	25
Debenture	80
Profit before interest for the year ended 31 January 20X3	60

    What is the return on total capital employed?

    A   17%   B   22%   C   24%   D   30%

38   The following information was extracted from the balance sheets of Z Ltd at 31 December 20X2 and at 31 December 20X1:

	20X2 $'000	20X1 $'000
Stock	100	140
Debtors	150	130
Trade creditors	125	115
Other creditors	60	75

    What figure should appear as part of the cash flow statement for the year ended 31 December 20X2?

    A $25,000 outflow
    B $15,000 outflow
    C $15,000 inflow
    D $25,000 inflow

39   In order to confirm that financial statements show a true and fair view, the external auditor should ensure that the financial statements comply with

    A   company law
    B   accounting standards
    C   generally accepted accounting principles
    D   all of the above

40   S Ltd purchased equipment for $80,000 on 1 July 20X2. The company's accounting year end is 31 December. It is S Ltd's policy to charge a full year's depreciation in the year of purchase. S Ltd depreciates its equipment on the reducing balance basis at 25% per annum.

    The net book value of the equipment at 31 December 20X5 should be

    A   Nil   B $25,312   C $29,531   D $33,750

MOCK ASSESSMENT 2
ANSWERS

DO NOT TURN THIS PAGE UNTIL YOU
HAVE COMPLETED THE MOCK ASSESSMENT

1   C   The directors main responsibility is to safeguard the assets of the business.

2   A   This is the auditors **primary** responsibility

3   D   Need make no adjustments

4   B   £11,200 overdrawn

Cash book	£	*Bank statement*	£
Balance	(8,970)	Balance	(11,200)
Bank charges	(550)	Credit in error	(425)
		Unpresented cheques	(3,275)
		Outstanding deposits	5,380
	(9,520)		(9,520)

5   D   £88,000

	£
Cost of machine	80,000
Installation	5,000
Training	2,000
Testing	1,000
	88,000

6   A   It proves the arithmetical accuracy of the ledgers.

7   A   The expenditure has been understated by £45 so the cash drawn from the bank will also be £45 short, giving a balance of £705

8   C   Accrued: £560; charge to P & L £3,320

Electricity account

		£		£
			Balance b/fwd	300
20X0				
1 August	Paid bank	600		
1 November	Paid bank	720		
20X1				
1 February	Paid bank	900		
30 June	Paid bank	840		
30 June	Accrual c/d			
	($£840 \times {}^2/_3$)	560	Profit and loss account	3,320
		3,620		3,620

9   A   £6,800

Gas supplier account

	£			£
Balance b/fwd	200			
Bank £600 × 12	7,200	28 February	Invoice	1,300
		31 May	Invoice	1,400
		31 August	Invoice	2,100
		30 November	Invoice	2,000
		30 November	Balance c/d	600
	7,400			7,400

Gas account

			£			£
28 February	Invoice		1,300			
31 May	Invoice		1,400			
31 August	Invoice		2,100			
30 November	Invoice		2,000	30 November P&L account		6,800
			6,800			6,800

10   B   £4,700

	Cost	Net realisable value	Lower of cost & NRV	Units	Value
	£	£	£		£
Basic	6	8	6	200	1,200
Super	9	8	8	250	2,000
Luxury	18	10	10	150	1,500
					4,700

11   B   Profit: £781

	£
Cost	10,000
20X7 Depreciation	2,500
	7,500
20X8 Depreciation	1,875
	5,625
20X9 Depreciation	1,406
	4,219
20Y0 Part exchange	5,000
Profit	781

12   A   12.5% $\dfrac{\text{Operating profit}}{\text{Capital employed}} = \dfrac{£15,000}{£120,000} \times 100 = 12.5\%$

13   C   73 days $\dfrac{\text{Debtors including VAT}}{\text{Credit sales inlcuding VAT}} = \dfrac{£23,500}{£117,500} \times 365\,\text{days} = 73\,\text{days}$

14   B   The measurement of profit

15   C   Preparing bank reconciliations

16   C   £2,950. 10 units at £45 plus 50 units at £50

17   B   This receipt will eliminate the insurance debtor and reduce the loss on disposal by 500.

18   B

Suspense account

DR	Discounts received	800	Opening balance	2,300	CR
	Closing balance	2,100	Cash receipts	600	
		2,900		2,900	

Discount received should have been posted as a credit, so appears in the suspense account as DR 800

19   C

Opening WIP	240,000
Prime cost	720,000
Overheads	72,000
Closing WIP	(350,000)
Factory cost of finished goods	682,000

20   C

Output tax 200,000 × 15%	(30,000)
Input tax 161,000 × 15/115	21,000
Payable	(9,000)

21   B

Missing accrual	1,500
Closing stock overvalued – cost of sales understated	500
Net profit overstated	2,000

22   A

Cash book balance	12,350
Bank charges	(170)
Direct debit	(230)
Dishonoured cheque	(110)
	11,840

23   B   Gas charges for two months have to be accrued

	DR	CR
Gas expense	1,400	
Accruals		1,400

24   C

Opening WIP	40,000
Prime cost	122,000
Overheads	185,000
Factory cost of finished goods	(300,000)
Closing WIP	47,000

25   D   £4,700 is payable. £700 goes to the VAT account in the balance sheet.

26   D   The cost of the equipment has been debited to the profit and loss account instead of fixed assets so both profit and fixed assets are understated.

27   C

1.7.20X1 – 31.3.20X2 1800 x 9/12 =	1,350
1.4.20X2 – 30.6.20X2 2000 x 3/12 =	500
	1,850

28   A   Net profit margin = ROCE / Net asset turnover
                                    = 24%/3 = 8%

29   D   Remember, employers NI is an additional cost.

30 **A**

1-2 months	24,000 × 1%	240
2-3 months	8,000 × 10%	800
Over 3 months	6,000 × 30%	1,800
Balance sheet total		2,840
Provision b/f		(2,880)
Credit profit and loss		(40)
Total debtors	50,000	
Less provision	(2,840)	
	47,160	

31 **C** Prime cost includes all *direct* costs of production.

32 **B**

DR		Supplier account	CR
Returns	100	Balance b/f	1,200
Payment	1,615	Goods	1,700
Discount received	85		
Balance c/f	1,100		
	2,900		2,900

33 **B** It helps in detecting errors. It should agree to the sales ledger.

34 **C**

Net cash inflow from operating activities	26,000
Dividend paid	(3,000)
Proceeds of sale of fixed assets	5,000
Taxation paid	(2,000)
Interest paid	(4,000)
Payments for fixed assets	(8,000)
Issue of debentures	6,000
Net increase	20,000

35 **B** A and C are expenses. Dividends are paid out of retained profit.

36 **B**

Window cleaning	20
Stationery	100
Coffee etc.	145
Staff receipt	(20)
Cash sale proceeds	(60)
Increase in float	75
	260

37 **A** $\dfrac{\text{Profit before interest}}{\text{Capital} (200 + 50 + 25 + 80)}\% = \dfrac{60}{355}\% = 16.9\%$

38 **C**

	Inflow	Outflow
Reduction in stock	40,000	
Increase in debtors		20,000
Increase in trade creditors	10,000	
Reduction in other creditors		15,000
	50,000	35,000
Net inflow	15,000	

39   D   Although GAAP is generally taken to include all of them.

40   B

			NBV
Purchase price			80,000
20X2		75%	60,000
20X3		75%	45,000
20X4		75%	33,750
20X5		75%	25,312

See overleaf for information on other
BPP products and how to order

CIMA Order

To BPP Professional Education, Aldine Place, London W12 8AW

Tel: 020 8740 2211
Fax: 020 8740 1184
email: publishing@bpp.com
website: www.bpp.com
Order online www.bpp.com

Mr/Mrs/Ms (Full name)

Daytime delivery address

Postcode

Daytime Tel

Email

Date of exam (month/year)

Occasionally we may wish to email you relevant offers and information about courses and products. Please tick to opt into this service. ☐

	7/03 Texts £20.95	1/04 Kits £10.95	1/04 Passcards £6.95	Success Tapes £12.95	Success CDs £14.95	Virtual Campus	7/03 i-Pass £24.95	7/03 i-Learn £34.95	5/03 MCQ cards £5.95
FOUNDATION									
1 Financial Accounting Fundamentals	☐ £20.95	☐ £10.95	☐ £6.95	☐ £12.95	☐ £14.95	☐ £50	☐ £24.95		☐ £5.95
2 Management Accounting Fundamentals	☐ £20.95	☐ £10.95	☐ £6.95	☐ £12.95	☐ £14.95	☐ £50	☐ £24.95		☐ £5.95
3A Economics for Business	☐ £20.95	☐ £10.95	☐ £6.95	☐ £12.95	☐ £14.95	☐ £50	☐ £24.95		☐ £5.95
3B Business Law	☐ £20.95	☐ £10.95	☐ £6.95	☐ £12.95	☐ £14.95	☐ £50	☐ £24.95		☐ £5.95
3C Business Mathematics	☐ £20.95	☐ £10.95	☐ £6.95	☐ £12.95	☐ £14.95	☐ £50	☐ £24.95		☐ £5.95
INTERMEDIATE									
4 Finance	☐ £20.95	☐ £10.95	☐ £6.95	☐ £12.95	☐ £14.95	☐ £90	☐ £24.95	☐ £34.95	☐ £5.95
5 Business Tax (FA 2003) (10/03)	☐ £20.95	☐ £10.95	☐ £6.95	☐ £12.95	☐ £14.95	☐ £90	☐ £24.95	☐ £34.95	☐ £5.95
6 Financial Accounting	☐ £20.95	☐ £10.95	☐ £6.95	☐ £12.95	☐ £14.95	☐ £90	☐ £24.95	☐ £34.95	☐ £5.95
6i Financial Accounting International	☐ £20.95	☐ £10.95	☐ £6.95	☐ £12.95	☐ £14.95	☐ £90	☐ £24.95		☐ £5.95
7 Financial Reporting	☐ £20.95	☐ £10.95	☐ £6.95	☐ £12.95	☐ £14.95	☐ £90	☐ £24.95	☐ £34.95	☐ £5.95
7i Financial Reporting International	☐ £20.95	☐ £10.95	☐ £6.95	☐ £12.95	☐ £14.95	☐ £90	☐ £24.95		☐ £5.95
8 Management Accounting - Performance Management	☐ £20.95	☐ £10.95	☐ £6.95	☐ £12.95	☐ £14.95	☐ £90	☐ £24.95	☐ £34.95	☐ £5.95
9 Management Accounting - Decision Making	☐ £20.95	☐ £10.95	☐ £6.95	☐ £12.95	☐ £14.95	☐ £90	☐ £24.95	☐ £34.95	☐ £5.95
10 Systems and Project Management	☐ £20.95	☐ £10.95	☐ £6.95	☐ £12.95	☐ £14.95	☐ £90	☐ £24.95	☐ £34.95	☐ £5.95
11 Organisational Management	☐ £20.95	☐ £10.95	☐ £6.95	☐ £12.95	☐ £14.95	☐ £90	☐ £24.95	☐ £34.95	☐ £5.95
FINAL									
12 Management Accounting - Business Strategy	☐ £20.95	☐ £10.95	☐ £6.95	☐ £12.95	☐ £14.95		☐ £24.95		
13 Management Accounting - Financial Strategy	☐ £20.95	☐ £10.95	☐ £6.95	☐ £12.95	☐ £14.95		☐ £24.95		
14 Management Accounting - Information Strategy	☐ £20.95	☐ £10.95	☐ £6.95	☐ £12.95	☐ £14.95		☐ £24.95		
15 Case Study (1) Workbook	☐ £20.95								
(2) Toolkit		☐ £20.95 (For 5/04: available 3/04. For 11/04: available 9/04)		☐ £12.95	☐ £14.95				
Learning to Learn Accountancy (7/02)	☐ £9.95								

Total ☐

POSTAGE & PACKING

Study Texts

	First	Each extra	Online
UK	£5.00	£2.00	£2.00
Europe*	£6.00	£4.00	£4.00 £
Rest of world	£20.00	£10.00	£10.00 £

Kits

	First	Each extra	Online
UK	£5.00	£2.00	£2.00
Europe*	£6.00	£4.00	£4.00 £
Rest of world	£20.00	£10.00	£10.00 £

Passcards/Success Tapes/MCQ Cards/CDs

	First	Each extra	Online
UK	£2.00	£1.00	£1.00
Europe*	£3.00	£2.00	£2.00 £
Rest of world	£8.00	£8.00	£8.00 £

Grand Total (incl. Postage) £ ☐

I enclose a cheque for
(Cheques to *BPP Professional Education*)

Or charge to Visa/Mastercard/Switch

Card Number

Expiry date   Start Date

Issue Number (Switch Only)

Signature

We aim to deliver to all UK addresses inside 5 working days. A signature will be required. Orders to all EU addresses should be delivered within 8 working days. *Europe includes the Republic of Ireland and the Channel Islands.

REVIEW FORM & FREE PRIZE DRAW

All original review forms from the entire BPP range, completed with genuine comments, will be entered into one of two draws on 31 July 2004 and 31 January 2005. The names on the first four forms picked out on each occasion will be sent a cheque for £50.

Name: _____   Address: _____

_____

_____

How have you used this Kit?
(Tick one box only)

☐ Self study (book only)

☐ On a course: college (please state)_____

_____

☐ With 'correspondence' package

☐ Other _____

Why did you decide to purchase this Kit?
(Tick one box only)

☐ Have used the complementary Study Text

☐ Have used other BPP products in the past

☐ Recommendation by friend/colleague

☐ Recommendation by a lecturer at college

☐ Saw advertising in journals

☐ Saw website

☐ Other _____

During the past six months do you recall seeing/receiving any of the following?
(Tick as many boxes as are relevant)

☐ Our advertisement in *CIMA Insider*

☐ Our advertisement in *Financial Management*

☐ Our advertisement in *Pass*

☐ Our brochure with a letter through the post

☐ Our website

Which (if any) aspects of our advertising do you find useful?
(Tick as many boxes as are relevant)

☐ Prices and publication dates of new editions

☐ Information on product content

☐ Facility to order books off-the-page

☐ None of the above

When did you sit the exam? _____

Which of the following BPP products have you used for this paper?

☐ Study Text ☐ MCQ Cards ☑ Kit ☐ Passcards ☐ Success Tape ☐ Breakthrough Video ☐ i-Pass

Your ratings, comments and suggestions would be appreciated on the following areas of this Kit.

	Very useful	Useful	Not useful
Effective revision	☐	☐	☐
Assessment guidance	☐	☐	☐
Background (Websites and mindmaps)	☐	☐	☐
Multiple choice questions	☐	☐	☐
Objective test questions	☐	☐	☐
Guidance in answers	☐	☐	☐
Content and structure of answers	☐	☐	☐
Mock assessments	☐	☐	☐
Mock assessment answers	☐	☐	☐

	Excellent	Good	Adequate	Poor
Overall opinion of this Kit	☐	☐	☐	☐

Do you intend to continue using BPP products?   ☐ Yes   ☐ No

Please note any further comments and suggestions/errors on the reverse of this page. The BPP author of this edition can be e-mailed at: marymaclean@bpp.com

Please return this form to: Nick Weller, CIMA range manager, BPP Professional Education, FREEPOST, London, W12 8BR

REVIEW FORM & FREE PRIZE DRAW (continued)

Please note any further comments and suggestions/errors below.

FREE PRIZE DRAW RULES

1   Closing date for 31 July 2004 draw is 30 June 2004. Closing date for 31 January 2005 draw is 31 December 2004.

2   Restricted to entries with UK and Eire addresses only. BPP employees, their families and business associates are excluded.

3   No purchase necessary. Entry forms are available upon request from BPP Professional Education. No more than one entry per title, per person. Draw restricted to persons aged 16 and over.

4   Winners will be notified by post and receive their cheques not later than 6 weeks after the relevant draw date.

5   The decision of the promoter in all matters is final and binding. No correspondence will be entered into.